Fireplace & Mantel Ideas

2nd Edition

by John Lewman

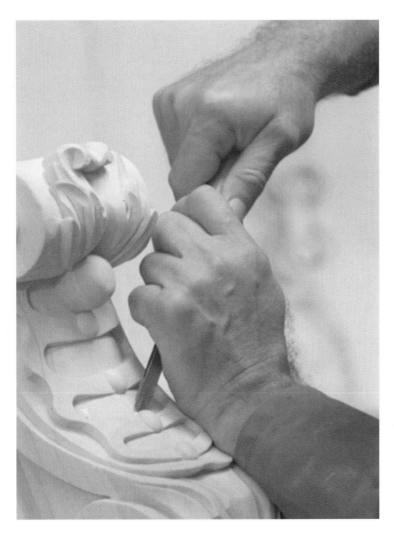

Fox
Chapel Publishing

1970 Broad Street
East Petersburg, PA 17520

We gratefully thank the following for permission to reprint materials and reproduce photographs:

Superior Clay Corporation/ Uhrichsville, Ohio

Heat-N-Glo/ Minneapolis, MN

Stone Magic/ Dallas, TX

Brickstone Studios/ Lincoln, NE

Superior Fireplace/ Fullerton, CA

Wohners Inc./ Englewood, NJ

Wally Little/ Las Vegas, NV

Greg Young/ Germantown, WI

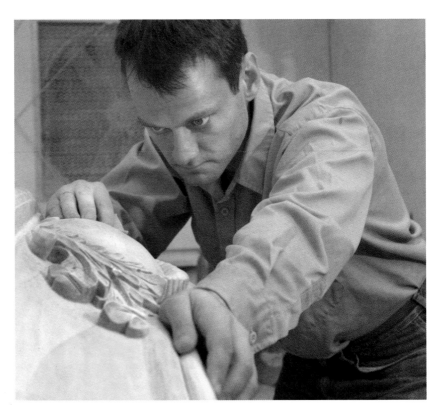

The **Fireplace & Mantel Ideas** *second edition* is published by Fox Chapel Publishing Company, Inc., copyright 2004.

Publisher:
Alan Giagnocavo
ISBN 1-56523-229-1

To order your copy of this book please send check or money order for cover price plus $3.50 to:
Fox Chapel Book Orders
1970 Broad Street
East Petersburg, PA 17520

Try your favorite local or mail-order book supplier first!

Printed in China

Acknowledgements

My personal thanks and hats off goes first to Alan Giagnocavo, publisher, whose foresight, patience and encouragement made this book possible. Without his support it would never have seen the light of day.

My heartfelt thanks to my beautiful wife, Cynthia, for teaching me Pagemaker, and for her many hours of professional coaching and design contributions.

Special thanks go to John and Robert Wohners of Wohners Incorporated. Wohners tirelessly and freely shared the fascinating written and photo history of their outstanding almost 100 year old family firm.

We owe a great deal to Greg Young for his creativity and willingness to generously share his skills and techniques.

And a very special thanks to Wally and Terry Little for sharing their original designs and work history.

In addition, a hearty thanks to Jim Buckley for his excellent Rumford Fireplace data.

Thanks again to each of you. You have contributed greatly to the success of the *Fireplace & Mantel Ideas* 2nd edition and have made editing this work a real pleasure.

Introduction

Our basic human need for light, warmth and security has developed in us an enduring love and a passion for fire. Over thousands of years and millions of experiments we have conquered the use of fire and made it the centerpiece and focus of our homes.

The fireplace and mantel are now the center of our social interaction, food preparation and comfort. And all of us find gathering around the fireplace to be the warmest and friendliest place to share our lives and experiences with friends and family.

Planning the place and function of your fireplace is one of the great joys of designing your living space. Based on today's environmental needs, you'll want to begin with designing for an efficient, heat-circulating firebox.

The period style and decor of your home is the next consideration. Calculating available space, the size and shape of the room the fireplace resides in, and the tastes and needs of family members also play an important role in your final decisions.

Expressing your individual style is easy with today's wide variety of fireplace mantels and surrounds. You can begin your interior planning with the mantel. Choosing a dramatic design can dictate your style, emphasize a theme, or add an element of interest and surprise to the interior of any room.

Ranging in price from moderate to exotic, the mantels shown in the **Fireplace & Mantel Ideas** book will inspire your creative efforts and provide both design details and sources for the mantel of your dreams.

We hope you enjoy the designs as much as we enjoyed creating and compiling them, and wish you the best in your endeavors as you explore the many possibilities available to you in this fascinating and worthwhile book.

John Lewman

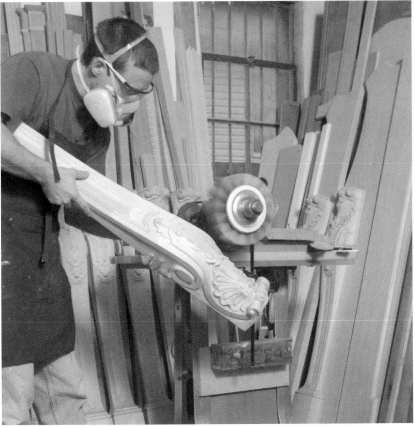

Table of Contents

Brickstone Cast-Stone Mantel

Chapter One

The Living Fireplace

A Brief History of the Hearth

Today you can easily realize your dream of enjoying a colorful, heartwarming fire while surrounded by a classically stylish and beautiful mantel.

The fireplace acts as the center gathering place of a home and holds a permanent place of comfort in all of our hearts. With today's new technologies your

High quality fireplace inserts for wall or corner installations are available from a variety of vendors (Heat-N-Glo).

options are plentiful. You can easily build your own fireplace and mantel or install one of hundreds of quality, made-to-order packages that will create a delightful focus in any room or space.

In the history of the fireplace, there has never existed such an exciting variety of designs, fuels and installation choices as exists in today's expanding market. You are going to enjoy discovering the wealth of strikingly beautiful, and at the same time easily serviceable, products and methods that when combined make up today's vast offering of home hearth options.

For all of us who enjoy the convenience of the TV remote control, there now exists a tremendous variety of automatic fireplaces that light beautifully with a click of the finger. You'll bask in the instantly enjoyable warmth of gas-fueled golden fires that can be lit while you lie comfortably under your bed covers on a chilly morning. The new remote-controlled gas-fired inserts burn as beautifully as any wood-fired fireplace and are completely safe and dependable.

You'll find that many of the gas-fired units will vent through any wall, without the expense and high maintenance of a brick chimney. Other more advanced gas units require no venting at all and consume all the gas fuel safely without any perceptible fumes or after-odors.

Superior vent-free inserts provide many options.

For the dedicated fireplace enthusiast who requires the tradition and realism of a "real" wood fireplace, we've included the details for building the famous, high efficiency

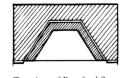

Top view of Rumford fire-box showing angled sides, shallow depth and back.

Rumford-style fireplace using Superior Clay's lifetime ceramic fireplace kits. The kits are expertly manufactured.

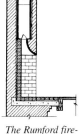

The Rumford fire-box straight back.

This striking design incorporates a high-tech woodburning insert. The mantel and surround are dramatically executed in quality ceramic tiles. A variety of themes are possible using this technique and allow for a striking design that can be built into almost any decor (Heat-N-Glo).

In **Fireplace & Mantel Ideas** you will find that whatever style of decor you choose as a theme, we've included ideas and the technology to help you realize your vision with spectacular flair and serviceability. Factory-built fireplaces can be inserted into any wall, then framed with a mantel that complements the room's decor. A gas fireplace can be positioned in the center of the

This classic woodburning fireplace is complemented by a beautifully designed and high quality cast stone mantel (Stone Magic).

The Rumford design is extremely efficient and provides superior design oppor-tunities.

Also included are the new clean burn wood-burning appliances that

Woodburning inserts come in a wide variety of current styles.

offer virtually smoke-free and dramatically higher efficiencies than the standard inserts that were constructed using the old technologies. All this simply adds up to an amazing increase in comfort, convenience, and very real fuel savings from every load of fuel you purchase.

We feel the best news of all is from the freedom of design when using the gas-fired units that are easily vented through any wall. No longer is the fireplace limited to the living or family room. Fireplaces can be easily designed

to work well in the kitchen, bedroom, bath, library, den or office. The fireplace can be freestanding, under a window, or in a corner while fitting precisely into your design decor of choice.

A dancing fire adds charm and warmth to any gathering of family and friends. With today's modern fireplace conveniences, maintaining a healthy fire is easy, and servicing and cleanup are minimized.

kitchen and framed with a simple easy-maintenance tile motif. A quiet bedroom space can be enhanced dramatically with the warmth and beauty of a freestanding ventless island fireplace. An unused corner can become a striking focal point in an otherwise ordinary room. Imagine the comfort of bathing in a bathroom that is lighted and warmed by the glow of a gentle fire. Beautiful mantel designs are available in the refined tradition of each historical era. Every theme is centered around celebrating the joy of the open fire.

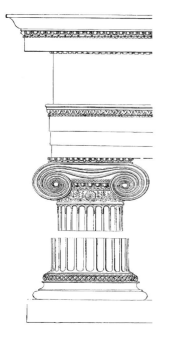

From Colonial to Contemporary, the fireplace is a pleasurable addition to the ambiance of any living space. Creating your own special fireplace hearth complete with the latest technological advances is completely possible. Come with us now as we help you discover the new joys of the hearth. Whether planning to build your own fireplace and mantel, or having it all installed by a professional, you'll find the journey enjoyable and enlightening.

The Classical World: Greece and Rome, 60 A.D.

The exciting art of fireplace mantel design extends back in time to the illustrious classical world of Greece and Rome. Our modern culture draws heavily from the influence of these masters of aesthetics and construction.

An important and influential feature of Greek and Roman design was the close connection

This early Roman living area demonstrates the classical forms and proportions of the era.

between decorating themes and their everyday lives. Religion, sports, business and pleasure were all captured in beautiful designs rendered in mosaics, tile, plaster and stone. They added decorative themes to mantels, walls and

floors. Colored marble, stone and tile were adhered to columns and overlays, creating dramatic fireplaces that from the earliest times were the heart and soul

Greek and Roman craftsmen were masters of the decorated column.

of every family gathering and celebration.

From the smallest hut to the expanding villas, the ancient classical craftsmen carefully constructed the joyful interface between man and fire. Their celebration of living is so primal that we still long to feel the joy of fire in our own homes to this day. Beautiful themes from these early times are part of our shared architectural history.

Byzantine, 900 A.D.

The Byzantine era speaks of unrivaled luxury, refinement and bold sophistication. The Byzantine period is the link between ancient Rome and the Middle Ages and

The Byzantine period designs are elaborate and dramatic and include Greek, Roman and Papal themes. This beautiful surround is in the living area of a rich merchant's palace.

was centered in Constantinople, where the lavish traditions of both the Greek and Roman world mingled with the opulence of the Orient.

Rooms were paneled with exotic woods and heated with magnificent brick and stone fireplaces. Gold and silver work abounded, as did green marble and red sandstone. Cast bronze enhanced designs and added the warm glow of exotic metals.

The overwhelming and dramatic fireplace became a common theme in palaces and villas. Great detail was added with fluted columns, elaborate carvings and beautiful sculptures.

Private homes enjoyed elegantly designed mantels that were the center of domestic activities and the focal point for study, reflection and rest.

Tapestries, wall hangings and oil paintings became common among the well-to-do and were often incorporated with the

The Medieval house was a dynamically active environment that centered around the hearth. The master and his mistress and children happily conversed with servants and visitors in colorful surroundings that were extremely functional and ruggedly constructed.

This dramatic modern design in cast stone captures the regal and aggressive emotions of the early Greek and Roman statuary. Modern cast stone mantels capture the latest features of the new technologies and are quick and easy to install (Stone Magic).

fireplace as the central point of interest in a room.

Medieval, 1300 A.D. Great houses during the Medieval period were bright, and full of life and color. There existed an obvious lack of self-conscious planning. Designs were robust and full of vigor and strength. Heavy woods, striking geometric patterns and simplistic carvings reflected the themes of everyday living. The fireplace remained the focal point of all activities of the home.

The Renaissance, 1500 A.D. Opulently rich with the magnificent works of Leonardo da Vinci, along with Michelangelo, Bramante and Raphael, the Renaissance established Italy as a world design center. Many of the most beautiful and important themes of interior design were developed in this astounding era. The fireplace maintained importance in interior design with the chimney piece as the most pronounced element.

Sumptuous mantels, tapestries, paintings, sculpture and furniture flourished in country villas and suburban palaces. Mantels were heavily architectural, reflecting ancient Greek and Roman columns, capitals and sculpture. Designs were often

The new prosperity of the merchant classes are reflected here in this magnificent living area heavily embellished with carved wood and ornament.

executed in magnificent proportions. Designs varied from the dark-minded and bizarre to the lighthearted and playful. All were executed with great detail and complexity.

The Age of the Baroque, 1600 A.D. The seventeenth century was the beginning of modern concepts in interior design

This modern luxuriously carved leg reflects the tastes and styles of the Renaissance Era. A master craftsman of the Wohner family carved this masterpiece by hand for a mantel created for a prominent U.S. customer. The Renaissance Era is a rich source of design ideas that is regularly tapped by today's artists and craftsmen. During this period, the ruling and moneyed classes experienced a burst of personal freedom as old shackles of religion, poverty and ignorance gave way. Today's museums are replete with outstanding examples of Renaissance art and craftsmanship. The society's new consciousness of its place in the universe was expanded by the emerging sciences. These discoveries went hand-in-hand with the rediscovery of the classical civilizations. The greatest designers of all time are from this era. Men like Leonardo da Vinci, Michelangelo, Bramante and Raphael each left us a priceless legacy of masterfully aesthetic and beautifully emotional craftsmanship.

and furnishings. The theme of the Baroque interior was to create a magnificent background for social events. Furnishings and decor began to reflect social status and stability. Each element of the room was designed to work with all the other elements to obtain an overall harmony of design. The fireplace became even more reinforced as the center of life in an active room.

The grandly designed themes of the era were a combination of Classical Roman and Papal (Catholic) origin. The chimney piece of the Renaissance protruded too much into the social scenes of the Baroque society, and began to recede. After plasterwork, the most characteristic medium was sculpting and wood carving, which reached unequalled perfection in the English designs for estates and villas crafted by Grinling Gibbons. Fireplace mantels were designed and executed as magnificently carved surrounds, very

The Great Houses of the Baroque period were decorated with beautifully detailed oak panels surrounding an elaborate and overwhelming mantel. Many of the designs include naturalistic motifs such as massively carved fruit, swelling curves and elaborate furnishings and tapestries.

similar to what is found in many late nineteenth century and today's modern homes.

The Rococo Style, 1700 A.D. is the last original expression of

The Wohner family designed and built this hand-carved example of a Renaissance fireplace and surround. The woodburning firebox includes optional glass doors and fireproof steel sliding screens operated by a drawstring.

the aristocratic ideal in European art. Its sources are complex, and both the Italians and French claim to be its creators. Its first appearance in interior design was definitely in France. Naturalistic designs in the form of seashell motifs and arabesques are plentiful in these overtly expressive and magnificently carved compositions.

Berain produced many engravings for chimney pieces that consisted of an elaborate over-mantel with a large central clock flanked by porcelain vases. Large over-mantel mirrors often faced each other across the room. This theme has remained a design element in aristocratic homes to this day.

The overall theme of Rococo is to create a feeling of extreme luxury. This can be achieved with elegant materials and elaborate

Rococo period mantels and surrounds were highly imaginative, if sometimes grotesque. Nature and human themes were woven into overwhelming statements that were intended to deeply impress. This sketch by an unknown artist of the era is a fine example of the exaggerated Rococo styling features.

A classical Rococo style mantel designed and hand carved by the Wohner Company. Note the careful balance of curve and line, and the extreme care taken in creating a dynamic and exciting surround.

design, or by a mixture of standard materials and skillfully applied colors in the form of gilded paints, textures and carved or stamped period appliques.

Neoclassicism, 1880 A.D.
This era encompasses a wide variety of styles and includes some of the most elegant designs of Europe and America.

The Empire style competed with Regency, Biedermeier and Victorian to be considered the most "chic" interior design statement of the times. All the Neoclassical themes were aimed at imitating the styles of art found in the Ancient World. This emphasis created international themes that were popular in all of

Europe and in the Americas.

The American versions of Neoclassicism were developed incorporating ornate lines embellished with ornately carved woods, overlays of gilt, brass and ormolu. With Yankee precision the American craftsmen shaped their timeless designs avoiding the excessive opulence of the old European masters.

Many of the Neoclassical styles are popular yet today and are found in many different types

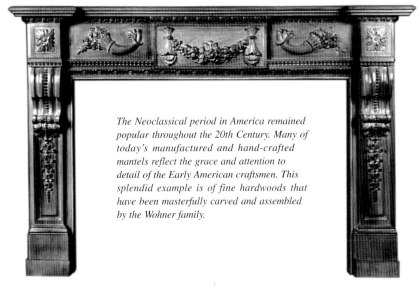

The Neoclassical period in America remained popular throughout the 20th Century. Many of today's manufactured and hand-crafted mantels reflect the grace and attention to detail of the Early American craftsmen. This splendid example is of fine hardwoods that have been masterfully carved and assembled by the Wohner family.

This unusual example of the Neoclassical style has an interesting and useful side chamber.

and sizes of homes in both Europe and America. The craftsmen of the late twentieth century especially favor the clean yet opulent presentations.

Arts and Crafts Movement, 1880 A.D. William Morris was resistant to mass production. He believed in remaining true to the materials at hand, and to the honesty of timeless design. The

movement was popular in America and was termed the "Craftsman Style." The designs were simple, popular themes, and sometimes included elaborate cutout motifs such as hearts or spears. Other motifs were inspired by nature. The later works of this

Both English and American homes enjoyed the delicate rendition of the Neoclassical period. The mantels were often a beautiful balance of brick and hand-carved and stained hardwoods.

A fine example of the overly ornate Arts and Crafts style mantels. Note the floral details.

period were the inspirational base of the dramatic Art Nouveau style.

Art Nouveau Period. In 1890 A.D., Europe developed its own version of the sinuous Art Nouveau style. Designs were shaped in a molten style. Many items had not even one straight line in them. Growing plant forms

This Art Nouveau classic is constructed of cast plaster. The dramatic curves and details are typical of the times.

abound. The German approach tended to be angular with stylized rose flower themes.

Art Deco, 1920 A.D. The Art Deco style dominated fashionable circles in the '20s and '30s. Luxurious and opulent, the look focused on leather, glass, lacquer, chrome and ivory. The forms tended to be sleek and stream-lined and were based on geometric shapes and motifs. Sunrises, trees, flowers, and animal forms exist in architectural stylizations that add emotion and texture to the themes.

Designing your own unique fireplace. This rich heritage of design from the various stylistic periods provides an excellent reference for contemplating the right mantel for your particular needs. Any of the period designs can be applied as a focal point in just about any room or home.

If you are designing using a simple, modern theme, adding a baroque or Art Deco mantel may be just the ticket for adding excitement and focus to your creation. On the other hand, a sleek and stylized mantel can create a quiet elegance in an otherwise opulent and luxurious setting. Consider using alternate materials and methods that are

The classic Art Deco period included designs executed in plain and exotic metals. This masterpiece is of burnished bronze and chrome.

adaptations of the themes and popular colors of the present interior design motifs. There are many possibilities. The choice is yours!

Right page: Late 20th Century Neoclassical

This current rendition of the famous Neoclassical style is easily executed and economical to build with common tools. The base material is high density particle board which provides a stone-hard and smooth surface for enamels or lacquers so prevalent during the era.

The individual components that make up the columns are simple shapes sawn on a table saw with edges rounded with a router or sander. The material is basic three-quarter inch thick stock available from most lumber yards. The bases of the columns have a sculptured look created by the addition of blocks stack-glued to give the variety of dimensions shown. The fireplace insert is an all-steel rear-vent unit. This particular style has the popular arch top. The classical design can be finished with a variety of techniques and color combinations true to the era. It can be built as a standard mantel height or with the ceiling extension as shown. This design wears well with almost any style of interior decor. (Crest by Brickstone.)

Heat-N-Glo Fireplace Products

Chapter Two

Fireplace Technology

Hearth Size, Location and Chimney Construction

With today's high-efficiency and cost-effective designs, heating with a living fire makes aesthetic and financial sense.

Heating with living fire appliances makes a lot of sense.

If you are like many of us today, much of your living is enjoyed in mainly one or two rooms of your house or apartment. A great advantage of the new fire technologies is the "heat-zoning" possibilities when using wall-mounted or freestanding appliances.

This modern kitchen enjoys an increase in efficiency and space utilization with a wraparound presentation (Superior).

These heating units are perfect for zoning the heat of your home, allowing you to concentrate comfortable air temperatures in the rooms that are used the most.

A big plus of the new units is their high efficiency. Many are more efficient than the standard home forced-air gas furnaces, and are ideal for supplementing your heating needs while at the same time lowering your heating fuel bills.

You can easily keep unused rooms at dollar-saving cooler

Superior developed this amazing freestanding fireplace that is completely vent free. These amazing units can be placed just about anywhere in the home.

The standard forced air gas furnace loses 25% of developed heat through the walls of the metal duct work. Insulating of the ducts does help, but duct work passing through inner walls is not accessible.

temperatures, while in the main socializing areas you, your family and guests are basking in the glow of a natural fire.

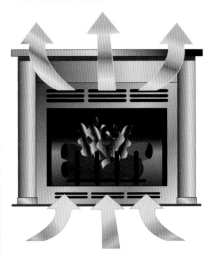

High efficiency inserts draw cool air off the floor and expel warm air from louvers positioned at the top edge of the firebox. Efficiencies can be as high as 80% to 90%.

The new technology gas and wood fireplace inserts are actually more refined and economical to operate than all but the most advanced modern gas furnaces.

A gas furnace system will sometimes lose a percentage of its heat through the surfaces of the ducting that runs from the furnace

Left Page: The magnificent ocean view is enhanced with the addition of a traditional mantel surrounding a Heat-N-Glo rear-vented gas insert. The insert is chimney-free and allows for the dramatic arched window that is aesthetically positioned over the mantel. Rear-vented inserts are available in both wood- and gas-burning models from a variety of quality manufacturers. Many of the units are EPA-approved and are high-efficiency models that rival the best furnaces in heat output.

The real beauty of today's new fire appliances is the incredible array of high efficiency installations that are possible.

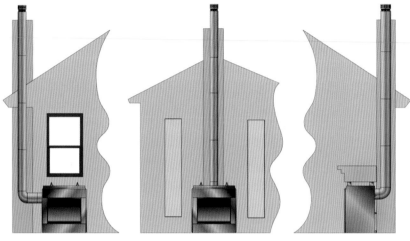

Companies like Heat-N-Glo and Superior provide a selection of venting arrangements for their fire appliances. Gas appliances are usually the easiest to place in a floor plan and allow for top, rear, left and right side positioning.

through the inner walls to various rooms of the house. The actual amount of heat from the registers will be reduced by up to 25 percent.

In contrast, the inserts on the market today have actual efficiency ratings of 80 to 90 percent. A big portion of the efficiency is due to the fact that there is no heat loss through ducting. The heat from the fuel burned is concentrated fully in the room

Dramatic styling beautifies this unusual fireplace. The all-steel insert allows for a safe and low-cost installation (Superior).

containing the hearth appliance.

In any situation you can depend on fully heating a single room. In many situations, two or more rooms can be heated if careful planning is employed.

The real beauty of the new appliances is the incredible variety of installations that are possible. Manufacturers have created beautiful fire appliances for any room in the house. Bathrooms, bedrooms, living and family rooms, kitchens, dens, home offices, basement areas, garages, even outdoor entertainment areas such as

decks and patios can all benefit from the installation of a real fire appliance.

If you are considering the cost of a real fire appliance in comparison to the resale value of your

Your creativity has no limits with the new technology. Corner designs can be executed in a number of stylish and successful executions. Your fireplace can truly be tailored to fit your needs.

home, you'll usually find that each added appliance will increase your home's value far beyond the cost of installation.

Brickstone Studios designed and built this magnificent cast stone fireplace mantel and relief mural. The design fits perfectly with the Corinthian theme of the decor. Brickstone mantels are well engineered and are of extremely high quality for generations of enjoyment.

And in addition to being a great investment, you'll daily enjoy relaxing in the glow and warmth of a living fire. What's more, you can design the installation of your dreams drawing from the incredible array of fireboxes and surrounds to create a dramatic focus to the family's favorite living spaces in your home.

How to calculate the correct output and dimensions for your fireplace:

Size: Choosing the size of your heat-producing appliance is critical to the success of your installation. If the heat output is too great, the room will become uncomfortably warm. In contrast, if the heat output is inadequate to warm the room to a pleasant temperature, the unit could run constantly, causing a sizeable increase in your fuel bills.

The Environmental Protection Agency has certified many of the new appliances. The certification includes efficiency and safety specifications. We advise that you install EPA-approved appliances exclusively.

Other things to consider when planning for efficiency are your

Side Note: Stored wood must be kept covered and dry. Burning wet wood causes excessive buildup of creosote in the chimney and can cause fires and reduce fireplace efficiency.

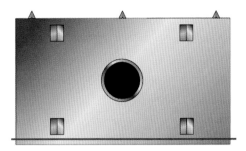

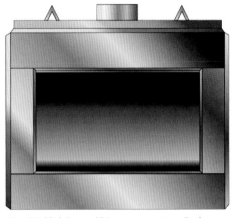

Economical Steel Wood-Burning Fireplace. In today's home building environment, cost is always an issue. The Superior KR models 38-3 and 43 offer homeowners the warmth and charm of a beautiful fireplace at the lowest possible cost. The clean-face design features no exposed grills. Surround materials can be installed right up to the front opening, giving the look of a traditional masonry fireplace.

The KR-38-3 has a 38" screen opening. Both use a space saving chimney design system. Options include an outside combustion air kit and a choice of decorator doors in a variety of style and colors.

home's size, ceiling heights, floor plan, and insulation factors. Also give serious consideration to who will be operating the appliance and how it will be accomplished. The type of fuel you wish to burn is another important factor when planning for the ideal size of appliance.

Location: When planning for a new fireplace installation, it is wise to take a stroll through the house to get a visual idea of where the new fireplace will work the best. You'll probably find that you would prefer to locate the appliance in a heavily used area like the living room, family room or kitchen.

Usually, some structural changes will be necessary to the house itself. The changes differ

from appliance to appliance. Taking a careful look at needed changes will help you decide on

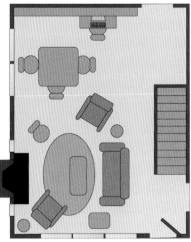

Fire appliances usually work best in the heavily used areas of your home and often become the center of family activities.

what type of appliance is best for you and your home.

The simplest installations are

the no-vent gas fireplaces. These need only the gas line installed through the wall or floor and into the units themselves. Vented gas fireplaces can vent through any outside wall.

Wood burning fireplaces and fireplace inserts require the construction of regulation chimneys. Be sure to discuss your needs with a fire appliance professional before starting your final installation.

It is a good idea to give the availability of fuel some consideration. If you are using a wood burning unit it may be best to locate the fireplace close to the wood storage area such as a garage or closet.

Keep in mind that heat sources

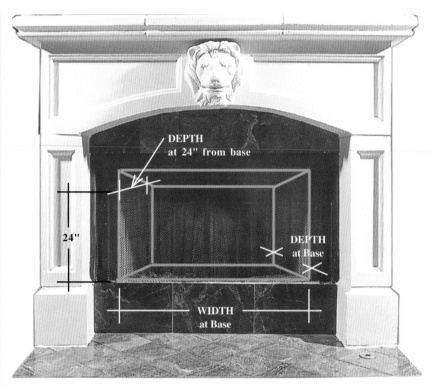

When purchasing a new insert for an existing fireplace, you'll need the width, depth and height of the opening. Also required is the distance to the back at a 24" face height (Stone Magic).

With the new zero-clearance fireplace inserts just about any mantel design is totally possible. Here a stainless steel mantel surrounds a new technology insert by Superior.

such as fireplaces work best opposite large windows that admit lots of room-warming light. This arrangement assists in evenly balancing the room's temperatures.

Fire appliances function most efficiently from both a social and heat efficiency standpoint when located in the main floor in the most popular gathering spots in the house. In this arrangement, units that include heat-circulating fans increase the efficiency substantially.

Be sure to locate electrical power sources such as outlets and junction boxes before your final decision.

If your home is two or more stories tall, locating the fireplace close to the stairwell will help direct warm air up the stairs to upper rooms, while pushing cool, second story air down to the first floor.

For those homes with exceptionally high ceilings, one of the new period-styled ceiling fans can assist in gently pushing accumulated warm air down from the ceiling into the living levels.

If your existing fireplace needs updating for efficiency you can easily install a wood or gas burning insert. Taking the inside measurements of the fireplace will be required prior to deciding what type of appliance to install.

Your measurements will need to include the height, width and depth of the fireplace opening measured at the floor of the opening. You will also need a clearance depth measurement. This measurement is obtained by making a mark on the face of the fireplace at a point 24" above the floor of the opening. At this 24" high point, measure the depth of the opening. This is necessary to calculate how high the back of the new insert must be to fit properly (see illustration above).

Planning for correct clearance calculations:

Each appliance type has specific clearance requirements. Both the appliance itself and its venting system has absolute limits as to how close the heated surfaces can come to surrounding structures such as ceilings, walls and furniture. These calculations are critical for complete safety while the appliances are in operation.

It is also a good idea to contact your Homeowner's Insurance Agent before completing your planning. You may be required to update your policy and also be required to allow for an inspection by the insurance provider.

Almost all manufacturers refer to the National Fire Protection Association's Standard 211

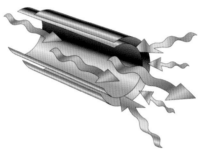

Most suppliers use mantel shielding insulation that permits the close attachment of mantel surrounds of both wood and ceramic materials.

(CSA or ULC in Canada) for design guidelines relating to woodburning appliances and inserts. Many of them exceed the requirements for operational

The chimney system is a vital element in the safety and usefulness of any fire appliance.

safety and offer special designs for reducing clearance requirements using items such as double-

Double-walled connector pipes and chimneys are available in long-lasting stainless steel. Special designs pull in combustible outside air while exhaling exhaust gases.

walled connector pipes and mantel shielding materials.

The NFPA standards are the best in the industry, and it is wise to adhere to the details.

Keep in mind that the data concern any combustibles that are against or near the fire appliance, including clothing, newspapers and magazines, and ignition-prone fabrics used in draperies and furniture.

Remember, for the safety and sense of well-being for you and your family, nothing is more important than a safe installation of the fire appliance.

Make it of the utmost importance to follow local safety and building codes. The codes can be obtained by contacting local state, county or city government offices.

Chimney System, a vital element: To keep smoke production and creosote accumulation to a minimum, to release dangerous fumes, and to maximize heat efficiency, are the important roles of the modern chimney.

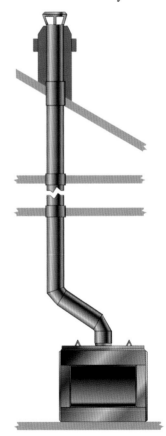

Complete chimney installations are available in stainless steel that extend from the ports on the firebox to the outside roof. Most provide clearance panels and insulation details along with well-designed chimney caps and screens.

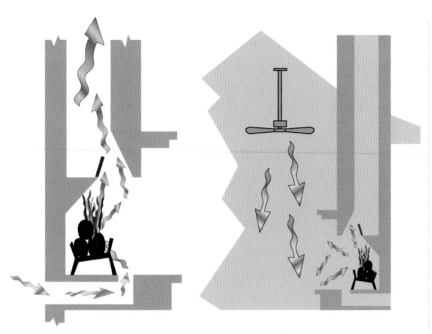

Outside air creates the proper draft for efficient burning with the fuel. If poor draft is experienced, the culprit may be a too powerful ceiling fan that creates a negative draft.

The chimney plays this vital role in the operation of any heat-producing appliance. Double-walled chimneys can do a lot more than just release the toxic exhaust gases safely away from the fire and into the outside air.

Another function is to create the draft, or air-pull that draws fresh, burnable air from outside the home into the stove to feed the fire. The air is then burned with the fuel and exhausted up the chimney. This "draft" is absolutely necessary for the efficient operation of any fire appliance. If the draft is not functioning properly, creosote is produced in damaging volumes, and an increase of environmentally dangerous smoke is released into the air.

Older chimney designs allow gases to expand and cool before they exit the chimney causing poor draft and corrosion inducing condensation. (Keep in mind that poor draft can also be caused by too low a chimney height, or from the negative pressure created by exhaust or attic fans that have been installed in heavily insulated homes.)

For your peace of mind be sure to specify EPA-Phase II approved chimneys to help insure the air safety for present and future generations. It's a smart move all around, and you'll benefit from owning a high-efficiency unit that uses a minimum amount of fuel for a maximum amount of warmth released into the occupied living areas.

For a safe and efficient chimney, consider the masterfully designed steel chimneys being offered by many suppliers. These prefabricated beauties feature corrosion-resistant flue liners, chimney connectors and chimneys. The steel is designed to endure elevated flue temperatures with lower heat requirements to allow for efficient appliance air intake. All this is accomplished with a minimum of creosote buildup. UL and UL Listed appliances are available that are rated "HT" or high temperature. These chimneys can operate at temperatures as high as 2100 degrees F. They also operate with enhanced draft, minimizing the likelihood of a blast of air coming down the chimney that can force smoke, dust and fire into the room. These chimneys can also be cleaned without moving the wood-burning appliance or insert.

Existing chimneys can be utilized when installing one of the new high-efficiency inserts. Their use will require attention. First, the chimney must be professionally inspected to ensure safe operation and compliance with the specifications of the insert.

The chimney may require a

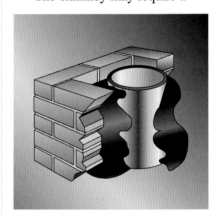

Poured refractory relines for old chimneys are possible with new reliner forms.

reline. A reline is literally a new liner inside the chimney itself. Relining can be accomplished by inserting a reliner form into the full length of the chimney, pouring reliner castable refractor material around the form, and removing the form. This method creates a perfect chimney liner and is a great solution for the chimney that is not up to code.

An alternative to the cast refractory reliner is the steel reliner. The steel reliner is placed inside the chimney and extends from the stove to a calculated position that is a code-specified distance from the outside surface of the roof.

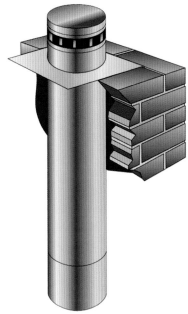

Old chimneys can experience new life with a stainless steel reliner that extends from the fireplace to the roof.

Your local fireplace store will usually carry a complete line of steel reliners. The dealer sometimes also provides a full service for casting the refractory-type reliner, or can refer you to a local chimney professional.

Chimneys are an integral and important part of your fireplace heating system. By taking care to match your fireplace with its chimney, you ensure the peak performance of the firebox and the long-term operating safety and security of the installation.

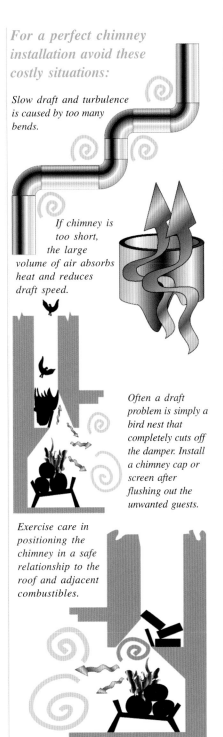

For a perfect chimney installation avoid these costly situations:

Slow draft and turbulence is caused by too many bends.

If chimney is too short, the large volume of air absorbs heat and reduces draft speed.

Often a draft problem is simply a bird nest that completely cuts off the damper. Install a chimney cap or screen after flushing out the unwanted guests.

Exercise care in positioning the chimney in a safe relationship to the roof and adjacent combustibles.

Considerations for all wood-burning appliances: It is always an advantage to vent a wood-burning appliance as vertically as possible. The venting can rise straight to and through the roof. Whether the venting is from the

center of the house, or up an outside wall, the chimney must extend a specified distance from the roof and surrounding constructions.

Outside installations can be the source of draft problems due to excessive cooling of the exposed chimney. This can often be corrected with a change in chimney length, or by increasing the insulation around the chimney. Other disadvantages with outside chimneys include more expensive installation and maintenance costs.

Venting from the inside of the house, and straight up through the ceiling is almost always the best design for woodburning appliances. There is an increase in performance with inside installations, and also a decrease in construction costs.

Several types of stainless steel chimneys are available for ceiling and outside wall installations. Double-wall pipe is available that allows you to construct the chimney closer to combustible materials than the single wall chimneys.

The floors immediately surrounding the firebox also need fireproof protection. The needs

This Heat-N-Glo insert is enhanced by a large off-floor fireproof hearth-pad. Ceramic tile surfaces are also ideal for floor protection.

for this type of precaution vary from appliance to appliance. Open faced wood-burning units require a large hearth-pad to catch sparks and cinders that pop from the fire. Even glass-doored units require the same consideration when the doors are opened while adjusting the burning fire.

Your local fireplace dealer can assist you in planning the proper hearth-pad size. For a stylish and classic hearth-pad, consider using ceramic, marble or stone tile. An endless variety of colors and textures are available that will go with any period mantel, and will satisfy any taste.

Chimneys must extend at least 3 feet above the roof where it breaks through the roof, and must

Exercise great care in positioning the chimney top to the roof and surrounding combustibles.

be built at a distance of at least 10 feet from any other construction adjacent to it on any side. Keep in mind that the dimensions listed are minimum dimensions. Your particular chimney may require a greater length for proper draft and appliance operation.

Chimney maintenance: The National Fire Protection Association suggests that all chimney types be inspected and cleaned once per year. Any buildup of creosote over 1/4" thick must be removed by cleaning thoroughly. Creosote builds up over time and can become a real fire hazard. A heavy buildup can ignite, turning the chimney into a giant blow torch that will destroy the chimney and often the house it is attached to. Firewood with a high moisture content can increase creosote buildup, so be sure to check inside your chimney for a few days after burning this type of wood.

In conclusion, it is best to call a professional chimney sweep to service your chimneys. They are fast and efficient, and possess the machinery and tools to do a thorough and safe cleaning.

Gas-fired appliances do not create a creosote buildup in the chimney. However, a regularly scheduled checkup annually of the burners, controls, venting systems and electrical connections is necessary to maintain peak performance, efficiency and safety.

In conclusion, with all wood burning appliances it is extremely important to keep creosote buildup to a minimum. To accomplish this, a robust, fully burning, self-sustained start-up fire is the best and safest approach.

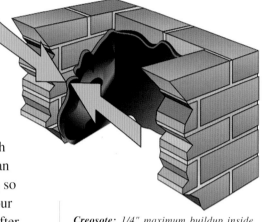

Creosote: 1/4" maximum buildup inside chimney allocated by the EPA. Keeping chimneys free of creosote prevents fires.

Burning wood with a moisture content of below 25%, and burning hotter, smaller fires will substantially reduce the creosote buildup in your chimney. If fire dies, restart using kindling to maintain proper chimney temperatures and draft.

In addition, ash removal is a critical maintenance requirement of all wood-burning appliances. You can stir old ashes among the hot ashes to burn them more thoroughly, thus reducing the volume of ash to be disposed of. Always store ash in a metal container with a secure lid, on fireproof surfaces, and away from flammable materials. Remember, cooled ash is dense in lime and potash, and makes a great garden fertilizer for healthy compost piles.

Common Fireplace Terms

Understanding these terms will insure that you and the professionals understand each other, and will also increase the quality, efficiency and economy of your installation. It will also help increase your confidence as you begin planning for your fireplace installation.

When discussing your firebox needs with the professionals, one of the most used of the acronyms is the AFUE, or the Annual Fuel Utilization Efficiency developed by the U.S. Department of Energy. The higher the AFUE rating, the more efficient the appliance. The rating reflects the heat output compared to the fuel input.

Most appliances will have a published BTU Output, which is a good measuring device when calculating the amount of heat required to warm a specific area. (A BTU is the amount of energy required to heat one pint of water 1 degree Fahrenheit.)

BTU Input is an important consideration for a gas appliance, and indicates the amount of fuel consumed in one hour. To calculate the appliance's efficiency, you simply divide the BTU Output by the BTU Input.

Burn Time represents the amount of wood fuel burned by an appliance with one fuel load. For example, you'll need this info when fueling up for long-term fires that are expected to burn throughout the night.

Catalytic Combustor is a wood-fireplace appliance accessory that helps your fuel burn cleanly and efficiently. They are a replacement item and last approximately 10,000 burning hours.

The Chimney is the passage through which smoke and gases escape from a fireplace and is sometimes referred to as the flue. It is usually vertical, and rises above the roof by a critical distance.

Creosote Buildup takes place inside the chimney and consists of deposits from the fire smoke. Burning wood that is not dry contributes to this phenomenon.

The cubic volume of a woodburning appliance is measured in Firebox Capacity, and is needed when calculating how much wood can be inserted for a full load.

The Fireplace or Firebox is an open recess for holding a fire at the base of a chimney and is sometimes incorrectly referred to as the hearth.

Fireplace Inserts are manufactured fireboxes that are inserted into existing fireplaces to increase efficiency and safety. Gas and woodburning types are available.

The Hearth is the floor of a fireplace, usually extending into the room and is paved with brick, flagstone or cement. It is sometimes raised above the room floor.

Heating Capacity is calculated to reflect the number of square feet or cubic feet of actual living space that can be heated by the appliance.

The Overall Efficiency of a woodburning appliance is calculated by averaging the combustion and heat transfer efficiencies. The highest published efficiencies reflect the most economical to operate woodburning appliances.

The Oregon Department of Environmental Quality has created charts that are easy to use and that will save you a lot of figuring. Note: The type and condition of the wood you are burning will effect efficiency.

The economic efficiency of operating a gas appliance is expressed as the Steady State Efficiency, which reflects how economically the fuel is transferred into heat.

The Vented Fireplace Insert requires a chimney or exhaust for smoke and fumes. Top vented, side vented and rear vented styles are available.

A No Vent Fireplace is designed for the safe use of all combustible materials with no fumes. These devices require no chimney, flue or exhaust ports and can be placed in almost any environment.

Step-by-Step Fireplace Installation for Placement in Existing Rooms

Some advance planning can make most any do-it-yourself fireplace installation easy and fun. Pre-planning, combined with a few dozen spare-time hours will provide you, your family and friends the comfort and warmth of a real fire.

Sharing your planning with your local fireplace dealer will ensure a safe installation that will meet all local building codes and requirements.

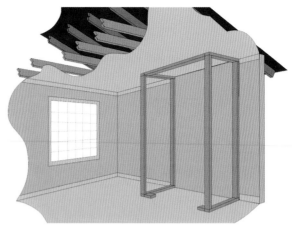

3. Using standard 2" x 4" studs, frame in the outside area of the installation. The two short blocks on the floor actually bump up against the steel firebox. The width between them equals the width of the firebox.

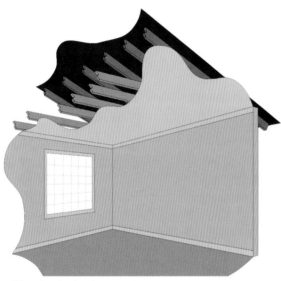

1. Planning begins by targeting a desired location for the fireplace. Locating the installation close to a large window will help offset the heat loss from large areas of exposed glass. Next, obtain proper building permits.

4. Set the insert without the chimney in place ensuring that all suggested clearances are allowed for. Install the optional outside combustible air kit. Secure the firebox solidly to the frame and floor.

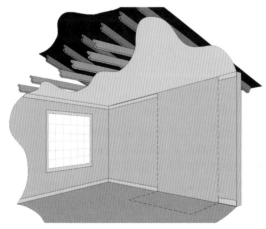

2. Prepare the work area by removing molding and trim based on the fireplace installation dimensions. Next, use masking tape to mark off the exact area of the installation on the floor, ceiling and walls.

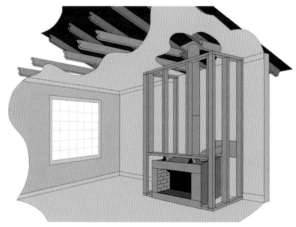

5. Make saw cuts to ceiling and roof members carefully following the manufacturer's guidelines and local building codes provided when obtaining the building permits. Complete the framework and install the chimney.

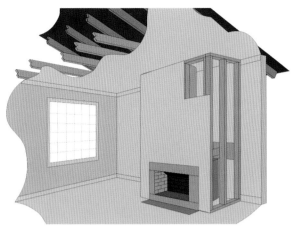

6. Many modern fireboxes allow for zero-clearance installation of surrounding building materials. Continue by applying drywall or paneling to the framework as shown. Finish drywall by taping, spackling and sanding.

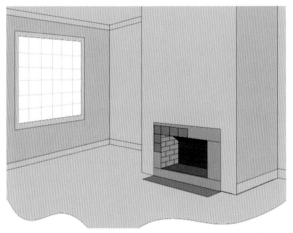

7. Following the completion of the wall surface installation, the matching molding and trim is added to the new fireplace area. This installation features a ceramic tile surround applied around the opening.

8. This do-it-yourself mantel is designed for easy construction and can be cut from standard high density particle board, pine or hardwood. All cuts can be made on a standard table or radial arm saw.

9. The simplicity of this design is timeless, and is appropriate for a variety of installations. The unit is assembled and finishes applied prior to attaching it to the wall surrounding the firebox.

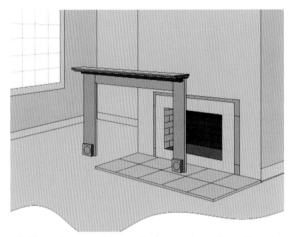

10. Next, the mantel is attached securely to the wall and framework that immediately surrounds the firebox. There are a large variety of fireplace mantels and surrounds that can be incorporated with this scheme.

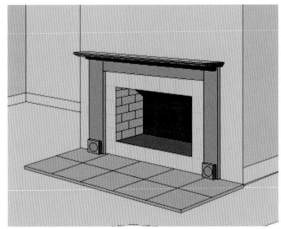

11. The finished custom installation features a steel firebox with actual refractory brick in the fire chamber giving an authentic aura to a dramatic installation. Mantels can be chosen from a wide variety of designs.

Superior Fireplace Company

Chapter Three

Wood-Fired Fireplaces

Traditional and High-Efficiency Woodburning Fireplaces

The latest firebox designs are better than ever and provide a variety of attractive options. Many surpass even the EPA's high quality standards.

For the purist, the masonry or steel traditional woodburning fireplace is economical to install and provides a beautiful and natural fire.

The Environmental Protection Agency has had a tremendously positive impact on the quality and efficiency of heating appliances. Uncertified appliances have about a 50% overall efficiency, while EPA-certified appliances all have a 70% or higher rating, while at the same time reduce pollution by 85%, and with woodburners, reduce refueling costs up to 30%. Another real plus is the increased cleanliness and ease of maintenance of the new designs.

The EPA applied the restrictions to woodburning appliances to help preserve the environment. In one five-year period, the certified appliances burned 700,000 less cords of wood than would have been burned with regular units, saving a forest consisting of thousands of acres.

700,000 cords of wood saved in five year period.

This reduced the amount of pollutants released into the air by over 400,000 tons!

When shopping for a new appliance, keep in mind that the retailer can only display and sell catalytic appliances that release a maximum of 4.1 grams per hour, and noncatalytic units that release a maximum of 7.5 grams per hour. In some cases, certain appliances are not required to have an EPA certification. These include some furnaces, masonry stoves, masonry fireplaces, coal-fired and gas-fired units.

EPA restrictions reduced pollution by 400,000 tons in just five years.

Uncertified appliances that have a 50% overall efficiency emit high levels of pollutions into the air.

EPA certified appliances have 70% or greater rating and reduce pollution by 85%.

The traditional masonry or steel fireplace is perfect for glamour looks where beauty is the focus and the aesthetic ambiance dominates the mood of the presentation.

Superior's ESTATE is the largest factory-built fireplace ever offered. This unit is for installations of a grand scale. Its firebox is so huge that it can best be measured in feet rather than inches: 4 feet across the front, 3 feet wide across the rear, 2 feet deep, with over 7 square feet of interior hearth area. It is perfect for country manors, stately residences and luxury homes.

Factory-built traditional woodburners. In new installations, the standard manufactured steel woodburning fireplace and chimneys are a first choice for many homeowners who are installing a firebox for the first time. Fireplace doors are optional but not necessarily a part of the installation. This traditional approach to providing a living fire is the most economical to install, is safe and reliable, and does not require an EPA rating. Efficiency averages are much lower than the EPA-certified fireplace inserts. Manufacturers' installation requirements vary greatly from supplier to supplier. Check the installation literature provided with the manufactured fireplace to plan safety-oriented framing and

90%

10%

Traditionals are 10% to 30% efficient.

facing installations.

Caution: Some manufacturers require additional metal strips to be installed in front of and under certain units. Be sure and check out the details with a professional.

Superior Fireplace Company of Fullerton, California, offers a manufactured fireplace that is truly on a grand scale. The firebox is a huge 4 feet wide by 2 feet deep by over 2 feet tall. The design features realistic traditional masonry. The massive iron grate can hold a half dozen very large logs all at the same time. Superior also manufactures standard-sized fireplaces incorporating the high quality tradition. Efficient outside air kits are offered, as well as

Complete installation kits are available that include firebox, outside combustible air kit, stainless steel chimney, flashing and chimney cap. Most are zero-clearance and include a quality heavy steel grate.

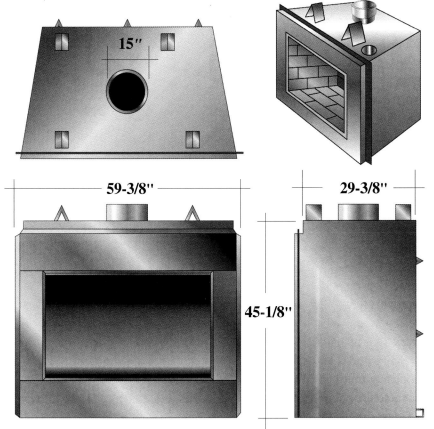

Superior glass doors are offered in a variety of high quality styles.

Superior's Estate manufactured fireplace features an incredibly realistic traditional masonry refractory. Recessed screen pockets and a clean face design produce a 48" x 28" rock to screen opening. An integral, masonry look, inclined ash lip is flush with the front opening. The Estate's massive iron grate is capable of holding a half dozen very large logs at once.

finely trimmed glass doors. This is one of the best manufactured alternatives to a large, custom-built masonry fireplace, and the beautiful masonry look of the firebox design works perfectly with stone, cast masonry or wood mantels.

Remember, when installing a traditional fireplace, glass doors can help keep heat in the house by preventing the warm room air from exiting through the damper.

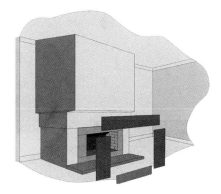

The Superior Fireplace Company installation shown at right can be reproduced by boxing in the fireplace as shown above. Once drywall is applied, sanded and finished, a high pressure laminate like Formica is applied in a stone or metal surface. The end result is a dramatically modern and easily maintained mantel. The new technology steel fireplaces allow this type of construction due to the zero-clearance features of the best designs. An alternative to the high pressure laminate would be a fine hardwood veneer with a semigloss polyurethane catalyst finish.

Superior Fireplace Company

The all-steel high efficiency wood burning fireplace or insert is a perfect combination of high technology, clean aesthetics, comfort and convenience.

They are always manufactured with heat-saving glass doors and electrically powered heat circulating fans. These latest inserts are easily installed into most masonry and zero clearance fireplaces, and provide a beautiful, heat-producing fire with a minimum of effort and a maximum of creature comfort and convenience. New stainless steel fire

chimneys can be installed. As an option, existing masonry chimneys can be relined with steel refiners, or with the poured refractory refiners that can be built to match exactly with your new insert's flue diameter. In this field, Heat-N-Glo and Superior are paving the way in innovation, quality and customer service.

The Heat-N-Glo line of woodburning inserts includes a clean burning system that is unique in today's market and has passed all four phases of the EPA Phase II testing. The EPA approval allows it to be installed in areas where wood-burning restrictions apply.

The wood burning high-efficiency units are always manufactured with heat-preserving glass doors, and electrically powered heat blowers. There are several quality producers of high efficiency fireplaces including:

Lennox
Regency
Heat-N-Glo
Lopi
Superior
Austroflamm
Fireplace
Xtrordinair
Mendota
Kozy Heat

The addresses of the listed suppliers are in the appendix in the back of the book.

Most of the fireplaces allow extremely creative installations. Various

Heat-N-Glo inserts work well in this quietly traditional setting that incorporates a custom off-the-shelf mantel.

venting strategies allow fireplace installations on an interior or exterior wall. Top-vent and direct-vent fireplaces are designed for installations in areas like the basement that cannot use a back-venting direct vent.

Heat-N-Glo inserts are available with a large variety of stylish surrounds. This model is a simulated marble look that is appropriate in almost any setting.

In addition, the appliances maintain indoor air quality and are not affected by house depressurization. The direct-vent designs have a sealed combustion chamber, using 100 percent outside air for combustion and exhausting 100 percent of all combustion products. This means that there is

Heat-N-Glo provided the high-efficiency insert for this grandly dramatic presentation. High-efficiency units provide adequate heat for large areas, and often are as efficient as a forced-air gas furnace.

no exchange of combustion air and room air and that no combustion by-product pollutants are allowed into the home. These fireplace inserts do not contribute to negative pressure problems so common in today's tightly sealed homes.

With fuel-burning efficiencies of 80 percent and greater, the inserts are clean-burning, use a minimum amount of fuel, and are cost-effective. Many even operate during electrical power failures. And if you are in a clean-burn area, many high-efficiency fireplaces will meet all regulations.

When planning the installation of a high-efficiency woodburning fire appliance, be sure to work with your local fireplace dealer to obtain all the necessary specifications and local governmental installation regulations.

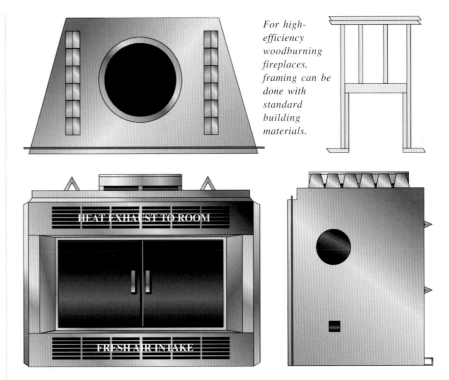

For high-efficiency woodburning fireplaces, framing can be done with standard building materials.

Several suppliers provide quality high-efficiency wood fireplaces and inserts. All are manufactured of high-grade steels and include tight-fitting glass doors. Features include intake and exhaust fans for efficient circulation of air. Venting can be on the left or right side, off the top or out the back of the units. The best woodburning units include stainless steel chimney kits and have absolutely realistic ceramic logs that feature permanent natural-looking hot glowing ashes.

High-efficiency wood-burner chimneys can exhaust from the top, rear or sides.

Some manufacturers offer high-efficiency units that are over 80% efficient.

High-efficiency units can protrude to the outside or be built into an inside box-in that requires no new foundationing.

Gas and wood inserts allow zero-clearance application of mantels and surrounds. This simple installation includes a readily available ceramic tile surround with a custom-made mantel. The mantel is of lumber yard materials and mouldings and is easily built and installed.

The Rumford fireplace is ideal for traditional installations. Note the stately proportions of the refractory brick-lined firebox.

The Rumford brick and mortar fireplace was designed over 200 years ago and is still the only masonry design that meets the EPA's environment-saving pollution standards.

Masonry Fireplaces: Of all the classic masonry designs we've reviewed over the past few years, the Rumford fireplace stands out as the most efficient and well-designed. Superior Clay Corp. of Uhrichsville, Ohio, and inventor and professor Jim Buckley have teamed up to produce the astounding masonry Buckley-Rumford fireplace kits based on the 1796 A.D. designs of the eccentric inventor, Count Rumford.

"With the assistance of the following plain and simple instructions, the chimneys will never fail to answer, venture I say even beyond expectation. The room will be heated more pleasantly with less than half the fuel used before...", Rumford wrote in 1796.

Purists love the Rumford fireplace. It was designed over two centuries ago and is still the only mortar and brick design that completely meets the EPA's pollution standards.

The following article, "Reviving the Rumford," by Jim Buckley was printed in the Journal of Light Construction.

A true Rumford fireplace is recognizable by its shallow firebox, angled side walls, and perfectly straight back. No fireplace heats better than a Rumford. Now, manufactured components make this classic design easier to build.

Count Rumford's elegant fireplace became the state of the art within months of its invention in the late 1700s. Unfortunately, even though thousands of Rumford fireplaces were built, few people understood the principles behind Rumford's design. When wood heat went out of vogue around 1850, Rumford's ideas were diluted by the furious competition to design and patent popular coalburning fireplaces. And shortly after gas fireplaces replaced coal in the 1890s, wood fireplaces virtually disappeared from American homes.

Wood-burning fireplaces became popular again in the 1920s – almost 170 years after the last Rumfords were built and by 1950 the modern fireplace had been reinvented as a result of the standardization of modern building codes. But by that time, a number of mistaken notions about the Rumford had become so popular that most of the fireplaces, including Rumfords, that are built

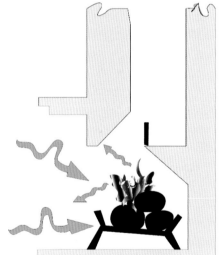

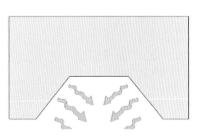

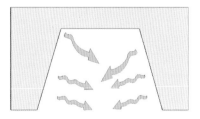

Rumford-Buckley Fireplace
Figure 1. The Rumford-Buckley design has a shallow back and steeply angled sides that radiate heat outward into the room.

Traditional Fireplace
The deep back and shallow-angle sides of the traditional fireplace radiate turbulent air and less heat into the room.

in America were modified in ways that were less than improvements on Rumford's design.

Most modern fireplaces are built as a nostalgic luxury, producing lots of smoke and not much heat (see Figure 1, page 29). But the Rumford fireplace is making a comeback. Its clean, simple lines are attracting more buyers and its effective use of radiant heat makes it a real fireplace to warm yourself by.

And while other fireplaces draw lots of warm interior air up the chimney, the aerodynamic Rumford burns cleaner and wastes less heat.

The Secret of the Rumford.
Science has come a long way since Rumford's day. Our modern understanding of heat and air flow is being applied to build Rumford fireplaces the way he designed them – with straight backs and rounded throats.

Compared with a conventional modern fireplace, the Rumford draws better, burns cleaner, and radiates more heat. The Rumford's curved throat and straight back create a steady draft in which combustion gases and room air stay separate and flow smoothly through the small damper. That's why the unique design works so well.

By contrast, the sloped back of a conventional fireplace creates a turbulent mix of room air and combustion gases. This design, in contrast to Rumford's ingenious design, cools the gases and creates drag, slowing the draft and requiring a larger damper opening.

Radiant heat. Rumford realized that the only useful heat a fireplace produces is radiant heat (in fact, Rumford coined the phrase "radiant heat"). The heated air from a fire goes up the chimney, but the radiant heat projects out into the room. Rumford thought the firewalls of a fireplace reflected the heat out; that's why he recommended whitewashing the inside of the fireplace. We now know that the fireplace walls, whether white or black, absorb the heat and then reradiate it. But either way, the angled walls in a shallow Rumford direct radiant heat out into the room much better than a deep, square fireplace does.

Streamlining. But shallow fireplaces tend to smoke, especially when they're wide and tall like the Rumford. To solve that problem, Rumford measured and recorded temperatures of only 75°F near the rounded throat; just 2 inches away near the back, we recorded 730°F! As we suspected, the room air coming in over the fire in a Rumford doesn't mix with the hot products of combustion. Instead, the room air acts as an invisible glass door that keeps the smoke behind it as they both go up the throat together.

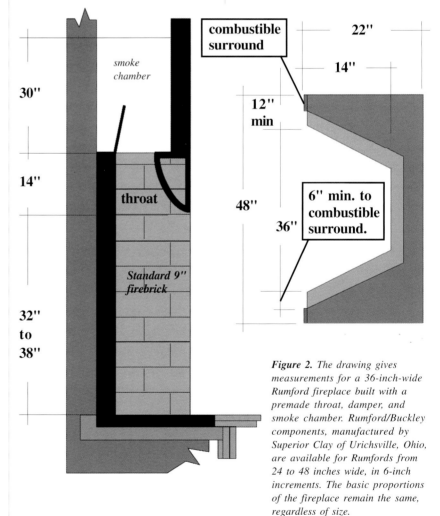

Figure 2. The drawing gives measurements for a 36-inch-wide Rumford fireplace built with a premade throat, damper, and smoke chamber. Rumford/Buckley components, manufactured by Superior Clay of Urichsville, Ohio, are available for Rumfords from 24 to 48 inches wide, in 6-inch increments. The basic proportions of the fireplace remain the same, regardless of size.

This laminar type of air flow – where gases move in smooth streams without mixing turbulently – reduces drag. That's why aircraft and automobile designers strive to create laminar flow. In the throat of a fireplace, laminar flow allows the smoke to escape easily into the chimney.

The Rumford is a real surprise for almost every builder. Most masons who build modern fireplaces won't believe a Rumford will draw until they see it happen with their own eyes. The rules are different for the two types of fireplaces.

In a modern fireplace, the fireback is usually sloped toward the front, casting the products of combustion forward. Incoming room air spills over the edge of a lintel and mixes turbulently with the smoke. Most masons will tell you that you need to drop the lintel 8 or 9 inches below the damper to create a pocket for this smoke and incoming room air to roll. Otherwise, the fireplace will smoke.

But all this turbulence is inefficient. The rolling smoke and air need a huge throat to get through. A Rumford fireplace operates on a different principle. The straight back lets smoke from the fire travel straight up into the chimney. The curved throat, unlike a square lintel, lets room air pass smoothly and swiftly over the fire and into the flue. The result is that the modern Rumford with an opening a foot taller needs a throat that is less than half the size of a regular

fireplace's.

Building the Rumford. The key to building a well functioning Rumford fireplace is to stick to Count Rumford's original design. His instructions explain how to carefully lay out the shallow firebox with a plumb bob using the special jigs he developed. Rumford recommended plaster to achieve smooth, rounded curves at the throat.

Nowadays, you can get modern manufactured components that save a lot of time. The method Jim Buckley helped develop uses a manufactured

Figure 3. The throat sits in refractory mortar at the top of a Rumford firebox.

throat and smoke chamber. Each of his components is carefully engineered and crafted for generations of efficient, safe and beautiful fires. The components are produced commercially by Superior Clay Corporation.

The firebox. Build the Rumford firebox using standard 9-inch firebrick and refractory mortar. Although a Rumford can be built to almost any size, the proportions stay roughly the same. Figure 2 (page 30), shows a 36-inch-wide fireplace. Rumford fireplaces are usually about as tall as they are wide, but you can adjust the height by a few inches. A slightly shorter opening makes the fireplace draw better, especially when

Figure 4. The cast iron damper mounts directly on top of the curved throat component of a Rumford firebox.

a small fire is built in a large fireplace.

The side walls of the firebox are angled inward no more than 135 degrees off the back wall. Use refractory mortar to lay the firebrick. The firebox walls should be at least 8 inches thick, so back up the firebrick with solid masonry. Pack any voids full of ordinary mortar.

Throat and damper. Set the curved Rumford throat in refractory mortar on top of the firebox (Figure 3, page 31). Lay up surrounding masonry to the top of the throat, packing the throat solid with ordinary mortar as you go.

The throat is designed to carry the load, but place a length of rebar in the first thick mortar joint above the front edge of the throat to provide an extra margin of safety. Set the cast iron damper in a bed of mortar over the throat opening (Figure 4, page 31). Make sure the valve plate can open and close freely. Close the valve.

Smoke chamber. You have some leeway in positioning the smoke chamber (Figure 5, above) over the damper. Line it up with where you want the flue to be, but check again to be sure that the damper valve can still open and close freely.

After surrounding the smoke chamber with masonry at least 4 inches thick, you are ready to set the first flue tile. Build the rest of the chimney just as you would any other chimney.

The Surround. As with any fireplace, Rumford surrounds should be at least 6 inches wide, which keep combustible materials

Figure 5. The Rumford firebox and smoke chamber is now ready for the chimney construction.

away from the source of heat and flame. Rumford surrounds should be almost flush with the wall of the room. Any masonry that projects around the side of the fireplace will block some of the radiant heat. At the top of the fireplace opening, bring the surround material just low enough to cover the edge of the throat, but maintain the streamlined curve of the throat.

This curve is like the leading edge of an airplane wing. You will ruin the air flow if you drop a header several inches below the opening. Again, try to avoid a brick surround that requires an angled

lintel to support the header, because that would make it hard to maintain the streamlining.

Glass doors. Rumford fireplaces don't need glass doors, but if you choose to have them, mount the doors on the outside surface of the surround so that the lines of the covings and the curved throat are not interrupted. Since glass blocks about 80 percent of radiant heat, open the doors when the fire is lit. The scientific data is not yet available to put numbers on the Rumford's comparative efficiency; but anyone who owns a well-made Rumford can tell you that lighting a fire in a Rumford is a great way to warm up a room. If you haven't tried it, you don't know what you're missing.

Jim Buckley, of Seattle, Washington, has been a mason for 15 years and has built more than 600 Rumford fireplaces.

Count Rumford was born Benjamin Thompson in Woburn, Mass., in 1753. He picked the wrong side in the American Revolution and had to leave suddenly with the British. For his work on the subject of fireplaces, the Bavarian government gave him the title of Count of the Holy Roman Empire.

Thomas Jefferson read Rumford's essays within months after they were published and switched to building Rumford fireplaces at Monticello. By 1834, Henry Thoreau's Walden listed a Rumford fireplace as one of the comforts taken for granted by modern man.

But wrong ideas about Rumford fireplaces were introduced right from the beginning by others, and have been passed along up to the present day. For example, the mistaken notion that the purpose of the "smoke shelf" is to block downdrafts in the back of the chimney was first put forward in 1796 by Thomas Danforth in an essay "fully explaining" Rumford.

His essays are out of print now, but you can still find them in libraries: Look for the Collected Works of Count Rumford, Vol: II, edited by Sanborn Brown. – J.B.

Step by Step details for constructing the efficient and modern Rumford/Buckley woodburning brick fireplace:

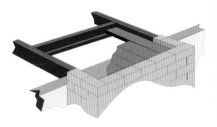

1. Hearth base and foundation. A solid masonry hearth base 4" thick should be supported on an adequate masonry foundation. The base must be deep enough front to back to support the fireplace and chimney. The face is typically flush with the inside wall.

2. Framing around the fire-place. Combustibles are to be kept at least 2" away from the outside of a masonry fireplace or chimney. The opening in the combustible wall is 4" wider than the masonry, with the header 3' above the top of the fireplace opening.

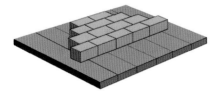

3. Inner hearth. Lay the fire-brick on masonry hearth base using refractory mortar. Make joints minimum 1/16" between firebrick. The firebrick inner hearth is just big enough so the firebrick box can be laid on top of this firebrick inner hearth.

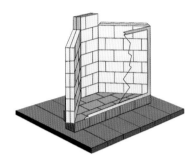

4. Building the firebox. Set, level and brace the steel frame of the glass door (provided with Superior Clay kit) on the hearth where the rough firebrick opening is positioned at a point flush with the inside house wall. Build the firebox using standard 9" refractory brick.

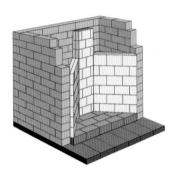

5. Constructing the backup block. The firebrick is backed up with solid masonry creating a firebox wall at least 8" thick. The bricks or concrete blocks are woven together at the corners for strength. Fill the space between the block and the firebrick with ordinary mortar.

6. Setting the throat. Thread the throat tiles onto a steel angle iron provided in the kit

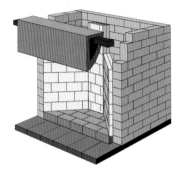

and set the throat as a unit on the block bearing surfaces. Align the bottom edge of the throat against the door frame template. Work refractory mortar into the joints. Remember, the masonry throat opening dimensions are critical.

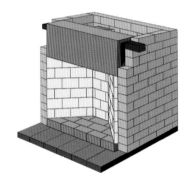

A full set of installation instructions is available from Superior Clay Corporation.

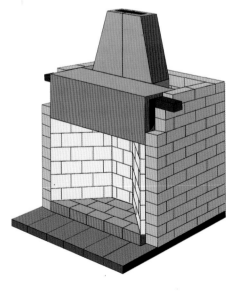

Many accessories, both decorative and functional, exist to make your hearth more usable and beautiful.

Fireplace Accessories. The timeless beauty of the hearth is enhanced by accessories that reflect the taste and life-style of the homeowner. Accessories also add an element of interest and surprise even when the fire is extinguished. There is a wide array of accessories available in today's market to suit every need and taste. Traditional items are plentiful and well designed, as are the contemporary and modern accessories. There are so many ways to accessorize to express your personality that you'll no doubt spend many enjoyable hours adding little treasures to the collection of keepsakes around the fire.

Protective Firescreens. Firescreens come in a selection of materials, styles and sizes to fit any fireplace opening. You can select from delicately designed metal screens and highly artistic etched and beveled glass masterpieces.

What's more, a stylish firescreen will add an elegant touch to your presentation during and after the fire. You can choose from one to four paneled screens that will protect the surrounding floors, constructions and furnishings from being affected by flying embers and sparks.

Fireplace Glass Doors. Prevention of heat loss is the major goal of any glass door addition. Doorless fireplaces allow the chimney, when the damper is open, to draw warmed room air immediately up the flue to the outside. Of course, the fire has to be completely extinguished before the damper is closed. Waiting for the embers to die out has caused many a homeowner to forget to close the damper at the end of the fireburning session. The open damper will literally allow all the room heat to be drawn up the chimney.

The glass doors prevent this after-fire heat loss. You simply close the doors when leaving the fireside. This prevents room heat from being lost up the chimney. It is wise to leave the doors closed whenever there is no fire in the firebox. Most dampers warp with time and do not close tightly. The loose fit allows a continual heat loss up the flue. Because of this, many states now require that all new fireplaces are fitted with glass doors.

Finally, one of the really useful features of every glass door installation is the protection from sparks, soot, dust and flying embers. Many designs help you control the flames with draft controls that limit incoming air.

Fireplace Grates. A wide variety of grate types are available.

Designers have developed highly efficient self-fueling multilevel grates that add convenience while increasing efficiency through increased air circulation under the logs. You can also purchase standard grates of cast iron or

welded steel. Grates keep the wood up off the refractory floor, allowing for increased air circulation and burning consistency.

Fireplace Gloves. This is a real necessity for the wood burning enthusiast. A good set of gloves with a long gauntlet  prevents burns, and keeps the hands soft and free from scratches and splinters from handling firewood.

Firesets. The woodburning hearthside benefits greatly from the presence of a well designed

fireset. Firesets assist in making wood adjustments and cleanup a pleasure. Many styles are available in cast iron, pewter and

plated or solid brass. Also available are bases and fenders in striking designs. Even though firesets are designed for wood burning installations, some will find the addition of a fireset to a gas-fired fireplace a pleasing and realistic addition.

Firestarters. Matches, lighters, firestarters of fatwood are all necessary luxuries for the woodburning fireplace enthusiast. For barbecues and campfires, you can start a fire in seconds using fatwood, a high-resin natural kindling. Combined with long matches or long-handled gas lighters, you'll be equipped to start ignition on demand.

Hearth Rugs. It is easy to protect your floors and carpets from sparks and embers with a fireproof hearth rug. The new styles are fireproof and come in a stylish variety of colors and textures.

Wood Carriers. Wood handles of dowels or canvas wraps make wood carriers ideal for helping you bring in wood for the fire.

Little wood carts on antique-styled wheels are also available. Fireside wood rings are also a smart investment, providing ample storage in a variety of styles and sizes.

Steamers and Trivets. Cast iron trivets are great for warming drinks and treats by the fire. Steamers help add moisture to the air during burning making the room seem warmer.

Bellows. For wood burning installations, these are especially useful when starting a new fire, or reviving a dying one. The increase of oxygen provided will instantly grow new flames.

Firebacks. Cast iron firebacks are available for wood burning fireplaces in both Early American and contem-

porary designs. Firebacks help protect the refractory materials in the firebox while at the same time increasing radiant heat.

Superior Fireplace Company High-Efficiency Gas Insert and installation.

Chapter Four

Gas Fired Fireplaces

High Efficiency units for existing and new installations.

Modern gas fireplaces are extremely clean and economical to install and operate. Many provide the ultimate in convenience using programmable remote controls. All are environmentally safe and deliver heat at extremely high efficiencies.

The authentic look and warmth of a wood fire is the standard for today's new gas fireplaces and inserts. And, with the addition of remote control, you'll enjoy the ultimate in comfort and convenience. Remember those cold mornings when you just did not want to get out of bed? A gas fireplace in the bedroom is easily possible, and you'll be able to start the fire without leaving the comfort of your covers.

The new gas fireplaces, logs and inserts are so realistic that you cannot tell whether they are wood or gas. Efficiencies are 70% and higher and equal today's best forced air gas furnaces using

30%

70%

Gas appliance efficiency is 70% and higher.

America's most popular and least expensive fuel, natural gas.

The great advantage to a natural gas appliance is the option of placing the appliance virtually anywhere in the home with a minimum of space requirements. Gas appliances are designed zero-clearance, allowing you to place the unit in the chosen area and build up adjoining walls around it. The newest designs allow for vertical, back or side venting. There are even freestanding vent-free gas fired fireplaces that consume all exhaust fumes and can fit virtually anywhere in any room.

The conventional chimney is no longer required with the new

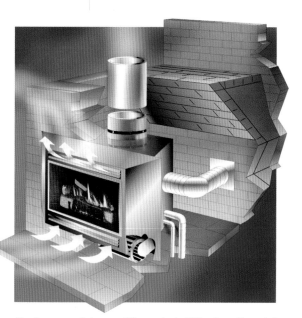

Gas inserts can bring new life to a tired old fireplace. For existing chimneys kits meet the most stringent EPA standards and come complete with new stainless steel chimney liners. Gas fireplaces are often more efficient then the best forced air gas furnaces.

gas technology. A real plus of the venting systems of today's gas models is the direct-vent feature. This ingenious design allows the outside combustion air to be

The new gas appliances are dramatic additions to any room. The dramatic improvements rival the heat efficiency and safety of the best forced-air gas furnaces.

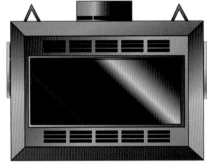

Sealed glass fronts and long-lasting stainless steel chimneys are typical with high efficiency gas appliances.

Gas inserts fit comfortably into existing fireplace fireboxes and are a great way to add glamour to a room while increasing the heat efficiency of the fireplace.

drawn into the heat chamber, and the exhaust fumes to be exited directly and horizontally through exterior walls.

If you desire a real brick look for the fire chamber to add to the installation's authenticity, fireboxes are available that are built using real refractory brick. The

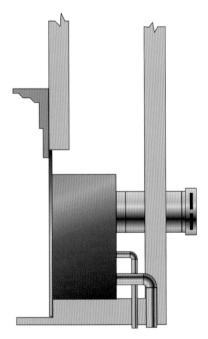

If you are adding a room or building a new home, gas appliances work well with new fireplace installations. Standard framing methods are employed with zero-clearance possible on most models.

authenticity can be enhanced with the addition of one of a wide variety of mantel choices that include wood, tile, stone and brick designs.

The designers have done their homework on today's classic styles. Finishes are of an extremely high grade and can be obtained in a wide variety of materials, textures and colors from enamel to antique brass. The logs themselves are so well designed only the expert can tell them from the real thing. You can choose from a large selection on wood species including oak, birch, and driftwood in many different configurations. The best designs include permanent burning embers and glowing ashes that completely mimic those of an actual fire, and that are never consumed.

The most astounding feature of the new gas fires are the flames

that equal burning wood in color and beauty. The new yellow flame designs have been tested and approved by the American and Canadian Gas Associations, and

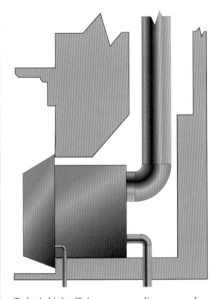

Today's high efficiency gas appliances can be placed in almost any setting. Top, side, and rear venting is available. Units feature warm air circulation fans for increased efficiency, and draw combustible air into the firebox from the outside. All have sealed glass fronts and clean-burn features.

also by the U.S. Underwriters Laboratories, and are completely safe. The latest designs use flame rods or refining fuel to create the wood fire look and have the added feature of varying color and movement that exactly duplicate a wood fire.

When installing any gas appliance you must have the assistance of a certified professional. Contact your local fireplace dealer for more information, or refer to the list of dealers in the appendix for a professional near you.

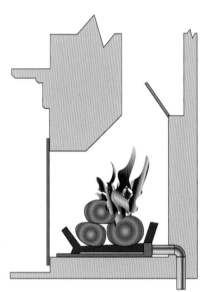

Gas logs are an easy and economical alternative for creating a maintenance-free gas fireplace from an existing wood fireplace installation.

Gas Logs are an ideal method for upgrading an existing wood fireplace. They're a great buy and are easy to install.

You can easily upgrade your old wood fireplace with a real wood fire look with one of the new, highly authentic Gas Log appliances. The units are considered decorative only, yet provide the authentic glow and aura

desired from a roaring fire. Installations are easy on you and your budget. Operation is simple, and lighting can be accomplished with a match or with a push-button control. And even though gas logs are certified as decorative, they will equal or exceed the efficiency of a woodburning open fireplace.

A great advantage of a gas log installation is the low maintenance required. There is no creosote buildup to contend with, and no bark, ash or wood chips to dispose of. It's a great way to enjoy the comfort of a living fire without the necessity of hauling and chopping wood. If natural gas is not available in your area, many manufacturers offer models

You can economically add to the appeal and convenience of a tired old wood fireplace with one of the classic new gas log sets like this beauty from Heat-N-Glo. The gas logs are as efficient as the old wood burner logs and require no maintenance. And the gas fires are as beautiful and warming as their wood counterparts.

that operate efficiently using liquid petroleum gas.

Gas Log design has come a long way since the early days of the artificial log. The ceramic logs are cast from molds taken directly from real wood logs and duplicate every detail including texture, ax marks, knots and color.

The realism of the gas fire is enhanced with vermiculite and rock wool applied over a bed of sand. These ambers glow realistically when the fire is burning, and add that final touch of realism.

Note: Always use a certified installer with gas appliances. Consult your local dealer, or refer to the appendix in the back of this book, for a dealer near you.

Heat-N-Glo, Superior, and other suppliers offer a wide range of gas log designs that accurately mimic popular woods such as oak and birch. Your friends and family won't be able to tell the difference!

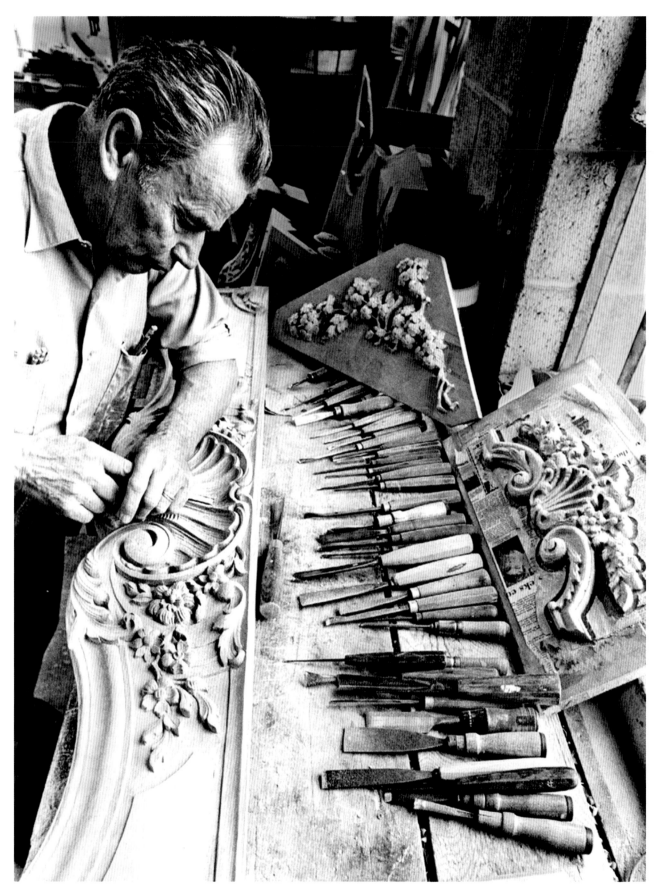

Master Craftsman John Wohner Sr. shown carving a Louis XV frieze in 1970. This frieze is a reproduction of one found at Versailles.

Chapter Five

The Mantel Masters

Contemporary Mantel Craftsmen and Their Works

Today's masters are preserving and improving on the old world magic of the classical mantel while creating wood and stone mantel originals that are stunning in their workmanship and design. Many are offering quality reproductions that are affordable, load bearing and maintenance-free.

The early 1900's Wohners woodworking shop featured many heavy-duty woodworking tools. Even at that early time, machine-powered efficiency was a strategy for producing affordable carvings.

There are many quality artists and craftsmen producing mantels of every style in a wide range of materials from wood to cast stone. The Wohners Family, Wally Little, Stone Magic, and Brickstone represent the variety of mantel producers that provide products that are beautiful, affordable and meet safety standards and most local building codes.

Wohners' has created a vast array of quality designs to fit with modern installations. The finest hardwoods and finishing techniques are employed to provide a masterpiece that will last for generations.

Wohners. The Wohners Family continues a tradition of excellence.

John Wohner writes, "We are very excited to introduce our woodcarved ornaments and fireplaces which exemplifies our many years of expertise in the woodworking field. Our tradition was started back in Europe in 1903 by my grandfather. His legacy was handed down through my father and was moved to the United States by him in 1956. Our reputation was built by creating the most laborious reproduction furniture, carved panel rooms, libraries, fireplaces, carvings, etc., which decorate some of the finest homes today.

The Wohners family success can be attributed to the close cooperation between family members. Shown here are the Wohner brothers carefully crafting a classic carving.

Now as my sons continue as the fourth generation in the craft, we have perfected our designs to allow their use by today's crafts-men. Through the process of

A member of the Wohners family assembles the mantel components following the carving and sanding stage.

machine duplicating, followed by sanding to a fine detail, we offer our carvings to you economically for the first time. Architects, builders, woodworkers, designers and the like will find these carvings a great aid in creating the look which they desire on a realistic budget. Never before was it possible to find ready-made carvings in such a wide array. I

know that, as a craftsman and a designer, this marks an exciting time in the history of architecture and design.

Every Wohners mantel design is carefully sketched and detailed prior to actual carving.

I look forward to helping you create beautiful period and contemporary designs in all kinds of tasteful applications.

Our carvings arrive to you unfinished and pre-sanded. The majority are available in both oak and maple, and some items are available in poplar. We are constantly updating our designs and reserve the right to make changes without notice. For large and/or historical projects, we can develop carvings for your needs."

Robert Wohners, President

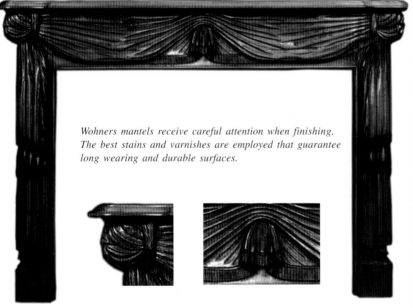

Wohners mantels receive careful attention when finishing. The best stains and varnishes are employed that guarantee long wearing and durable surfaces.

Stone Magic. Cast stone is a dramatic addition to any home. In this section, rather than talk about the versatility, the added value, or

This Stone Magic cast stone mantel is in a sitting area in a large family room.

the interest behind this maintenance-free choice, we'd prefer to talk about appearance. Cast stone simply has a breathtaking effect. Stone Magic is one of the first choices in cast stone when it comes to aesthetic balance, attention to detail, superior craftsmanship and quality.

Variations of style are endless

Each piece of stone is hand-crafted for beauty and durability. The craftsman is finishing the original keystone for the Bordeaux mantel.

with Stone Magic – from surrounds using only one profile shape, to complex designs achieved by stacking and fitting several shapes and sizes together. Many of these designs are completely buildable by the home craftsman. You can also have one of the Stone Magic designers create a custom design and installation to precisely fit your requirements.

You'll recognize Stone Magic's quality from details like cast-in corners, matching profiles in belly bands and surrounds.

To quote Stone Magic, "Stone Magic mantels impart a graceful and lasting elegance to any home. These fireplace treatments provide a rich, old world charm without the expense. Our cast stone has the look and feel of cut limestone, but is less expensive, load-bearing, maintenance-free, and we can do intricate designs at a fraction of the cost.

Most of the designs are suitable for metal as well as masonry fireboxes. If you need help making a metal firebox work, or if you have an existing ma-

Stone Magic's Windsor fireplace installed in a high ceiling family room. This wood burning installation adds an astounding touch of glamour to an already stunning presentation.

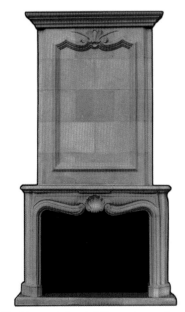

The Marquee's french influence is one of many Stone Magic floor-to-ceiling designs.

Stone Magic's Provence offers a range of sizes. The mantel can be purchased separately.

shipped and assembled. The special hardware required to secure the mantel and over-mantel to the wall is carefully engineered for lasting safety. The cast stone is so realistic only the most knowledgeable stone masons can tell it from the real thing.

The Provence is well-fitted to both high-efficiency gas and standard wood fireboxes and can also be incorporated with remodels.

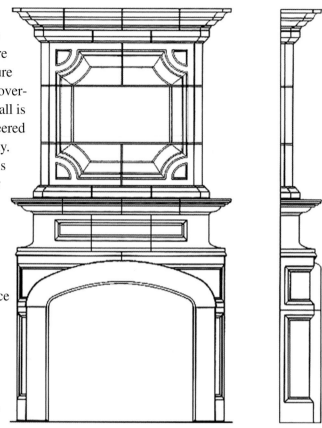

Stone Magic's Provence is offered in the Lower Provence and Petite Provence configurations. Firebox widths run from 42" wide to 65" wide.

sonry firebox that does not quite work, give us a call. We specialize in both the basic fireplace installation for private homes and cabins and the grand presentation for mansions and country manors.

Every detail of your wishes will be given the attention you desire. Remember, If it is in the realm of possibilities we can probably make it work for you.

The Provence is a fine example of design and workmanship and is easily

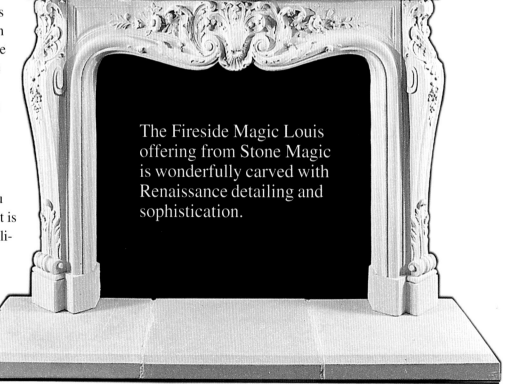

The Fireside Magic Louis offering from Stone Magic is wonderfully carved with Renaissance detailing and sophistication.

Brickstone offers finely sculpted and hand cast murals for placement above the mantel.

Brickstone Studios.

Brickstone incorporates the latest in technology with the care and elegance of Old World craftsmen. Their one piece, zero-clearance mantels are made of lightweight glass reinforced concrete which is a mixture of cement, glass fibers and water. The material is non-combustible and meets all requirements of the ASTM. They also offer NFPA Class A mantels molded using acrylic thermoplas-

tic polymers. All Brickstone mantels include mounting brackets and hardware. The standard firebox openings are 36", 42" and 48" in width.

Brickstone's creators have this to say about their work: "A medley of classic themes blends in a new and unique way to create Brickstone Studio's robust fireplace systems. Detailed to perfection, our handsome cast stone mantels form the foundation of an array of striking fireplaces. A truly distinctive touch is added with the Brickstone Limited Edition

Brickstone murals from top include Williamsburg, Lion and the Unicorn, Lincolnshire Roses, and Timberland Chorus.

The Lionsgate mantel is elegant in its simplicity and is designed for installation with wood, gas or electric fireplaces. The timeless design works perfectly with traditional homes (Brickstone).

1. Brickstone craftsmen carefully prepare the original prototype used in the mold making process. The resins used in mold making capture even the most minute details. This insures a high quality casting. The slightest flaw must be removed prior to casting to preserve the integrity of the design.

2. When preparation is completed, the prototype is coated with a high quality painted surface to preserve smoothness.

3. Following the finishing process, the surfacing material and the mold release agent are spray-applied to insure a perfect pull-off in production. Great care is taken to create and preserve a perfect casting.

4. A Brickstone craftsman removes the mold from a solid cast hearth. The cast hearth is maintenance-free and is resistant to scuffing or cracking. All Brickstone castings are designed for generations of use.

Murals that are ideal for crowning the Brickstone mantels. Elegant top mantels are designed to frame the murals, adding a dramatic floor-to-ceiling impact. Our three dimensional murals are handcrafted by master sculptors to create vibrant works of art that are unique in every way.

Call us for a copy of our portfolio or have our artists craft a centerpiece mural to your individual requirements. Our professional design staff can develop a custom creation or work to exacting specifications".

Brickstone's Lionsgate Mantel

Brickstone's Williamsburg Mantel

Brickstone's Corinthian Mantel

Wally Little, Master Craftsman. Wally has over 20 years carpentry experience from framing to custom home building. Ethics and the value of hard work and a man's word were instilled in Wally by his grandfather, Michael Pinto. Michael was a successful painting contractor and custom home builder from upstate New York. The Little Family relocation to Nevada in 1990 was driven by the building boom. Rather than become affiliated with an unknown construction company, they began their own carpentry business. Over the course of time the mantel business became the emphasis of the company.

Mantels were initially conceived with the customer as an active participating designer. In special situations they still are. However, one of Wally's basic five designs often fulfill the needs of most customers. All new mantels are truly custom units and use Wally's basic five as a foundation only. Variations in each design are executed with specially placed corbels and rosettes.

In addition, one of Wally's greatest assets is his ability to imagine the appearance of the

final product on site and to provide valuable input to the local customer prior to ordering. He is skilled at mentally visualizing and placing the designs on paper using his highly developed sketching abilities. A skilled craftsman's appreciation of the warmth of the color of the various woods and their required radiance in creating a

Wally Little of Las Vegas.

masterful mantel are skills that Wally acquired over many years of designing and building.

Wally's first Mantel. A customer requested a fireplace mantel to be added during the finish carpentry phase of his home. Initial design and customer consultation took four hours.

Probably the most intense portion of the four hours was the molding and carvings which needed to match existing decor. Working closely with the customer and witnessing his excitement was a pleasure. Later during the same year another existing customer requested a larger mantel. After extensive design work the mantel he calls "The Tarrytown" was developed. This large mantel, measures 72 inches between the pediments and is one of the largest Wally has built to date. Wally's mantels start at around $350. *The Little Workshop, 4290 Carolyn Drive, Las Vegas, Nevada 89103.*

This masterpiece, "The Tarrytown", was well received by the client and reflects the skill and workmanship Wally has developed as a craftsman. Even though all his mantels are built on the same design philosophy, no two are ever exactly alike.

Tile and grout designs offer a wide array of elegant interior solutions.

Chapter Six

The Basic Mantel

Wood and Tile Mantels You Can Build Easily

Mantel construction is easy with these step-by-step building instructions. The materials are economical to purchase, and are available at most lumber yards. The parts are shaped with common tools. Each design can be completed in just a few hours.

Mantel design and construction begins with establishing the overall basic measurements of the installation.

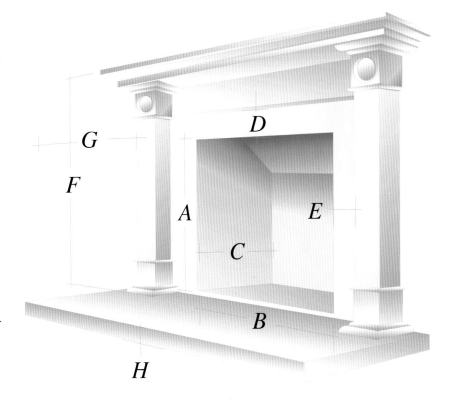

A/B/C: The height, width and depth of the masonry or steel firebox or insert is of first importance.

D: All masonry and brick installations require at least 6" of nonflammable materials surrounding the opening of the firebox. Zero-clearance fire appliances allow for close contact of flammable materials. Be sure to discuss this with a fireplace professional.

E: This dimension must be 12" or more when the flammable materials project out over 1-1/2" from the face of the firebox as in the case of top shelves and trim.

F: Most mantel designs look best with a height of 54" to 60" measured from the floor-level hearth.

G: All obstacles such as flammable swinging windows/ draperies, open doors, light switches and cabinets must be at least 30" from the firebox opening.

H: The height of the hearth and the distance of its edges to the firebox opening is required for completing the dimensioning.

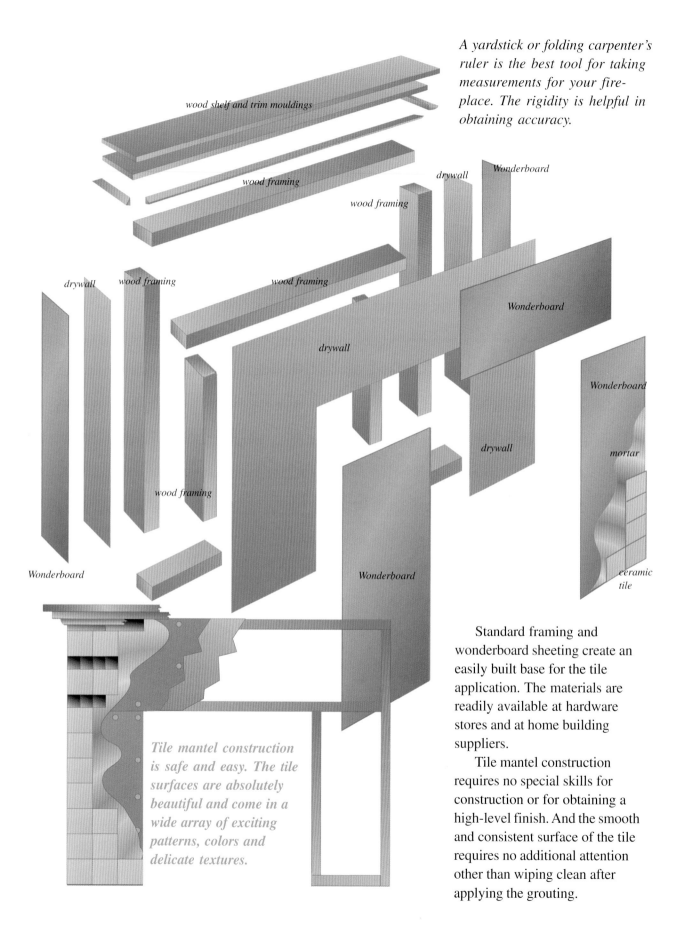

A yardstick or folding carpenter's ruler is the best tool for taking measurements for your fireplace. The rigidity is helpful in obtaining accuracy.

wood shelf and trim mouldings

wood framing

drywall

Wonderboard

wood framing

drywall

wood framing

wood framing

Wonderboard

drywall

Wonderboard

drywall

Wonderboard

mortar

wood framing

Wonderboard

ceramic tile

Wonderboard

Tile mantel construction is safe and easy. The tile surfaces are absolutely beautiful and come in a wide array of exciting patterns, colors and delicate textures.

Standard framing and wonderboard sheeting create an easily built base for the tile application. The materials are readily available at hardware stores and at home building suppliers.

Tile mantel construction requires no special skills for construction or for obtaining a high-level finish. And the smooth and consistent surface of the tile requires no additional attention other than wiping clean after applying the grouting.

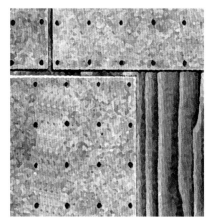

Step 1: The tile mortar bed is of Wonderboard, a portland cement material. Wonderboard can be scored and snapped to size. The edges are mesh reinforced and allow for a tapeless installation.

Step 2: Mark the layout for the tile with chalk or pencil using a carpenter's square. The layout lines must be at perfect right angles. Plan for cut tiles to be placed in hidden areas.

Step 3: Accurately position each tile on the floor before applying mortar to determine the best layout and number of tile needed. Cut each tile that requires modification to size .

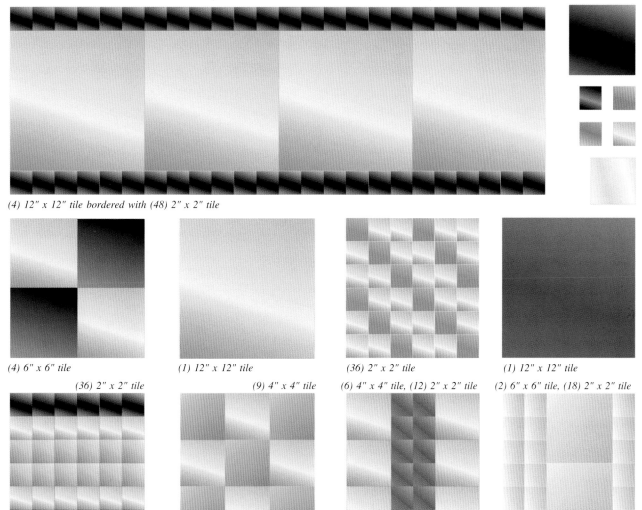

(4) 12" x 12" tile bordered with (48) 2" x 2" tile

(4) 6" x 6" tile

(36) 2" x 2" tile

(1) 12" x 12" tile

(9) 4" x 4" tile

(36) 2" x 2" tile

(6) 4" x 4" tile, (12) 2" x 2" tile

(1) 12" x 12" tile

(2) 6" x 6" tile, (18) 2" x 2" tile

Step 4: Apply bonding materials with notched trowel held at 45 degrees. Do not spread more bonding adhesive than can be tiled in fifteen minutes. Place tile with slight twisting motion.

Step 5: If needed, use tile spacers for alignment. Make final adjustments of each tile and beat into place with a block of wood and rubber mallet. Wait 48 to 72 hours before grouting.

Step 6: Remove spacers from application. Using rubber float, spread grout firmly over surface and tightly into joints. Work in small sections. Smooth and finish grouting with damp towel.

Tile mantels work well in areas where shallow-depth mantel shelves are required. This shelf is only 6" from front to back.

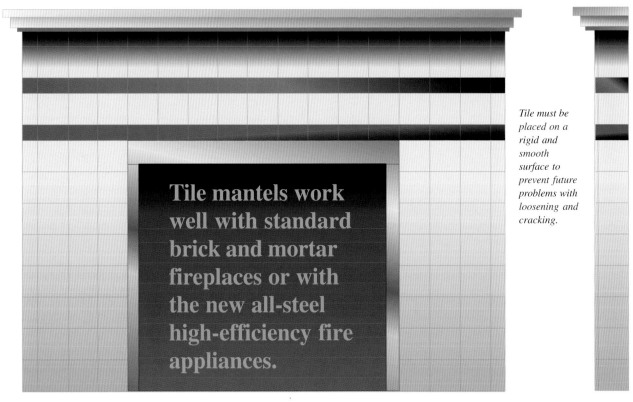

Tile mantels work well with standard brick and mortar fireplaces or with the new all-steel high-efficiency fire appliances.

Tile must be placed on a rigid and smooth surface to prevent future problems with loosening and cracking.

Tile mantels are easily kept beautiful and maintenance free by sealing the grout for protection against mildew, stains, scuffing and marring.

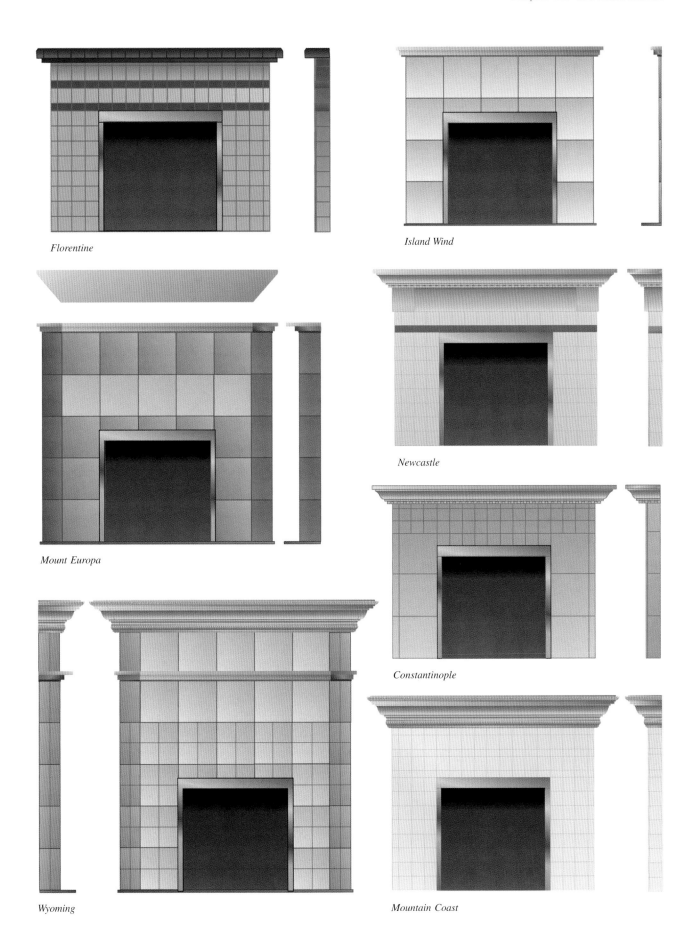

Florentine

Island Wind

Mount Europa

Newcastle

Constantinople

Wyoming

Mountain Coast

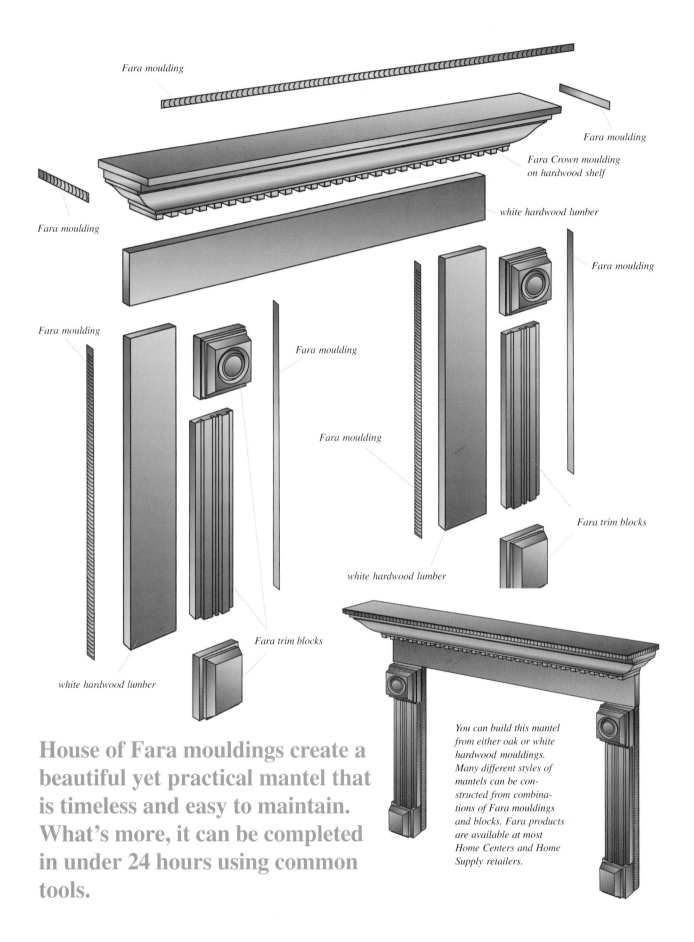

Fara moulding

Fara moulding

Fara Crown moulding on hardwood shelf

white hardwood lumber

Fara moulding

Fara moulding

Fara moulding

Fara moulding

Fara moulding

Fara moulding

Fara trim blocks

white hardwood lumber

Fara trim blocks

white hardwood lumber

House of Fara mouldings create a beautiful yet practical mantel that is timeless and easy to maintain. What's more, it can be completed in under 24 hours using common tools.

You can build this mantel from either oak or white hardwood mouldings. Many different styles of mantels can be constructed from combinations of Fara mouldings and blocks. Fara products are available at most Home Centers and Home Supply retailers.

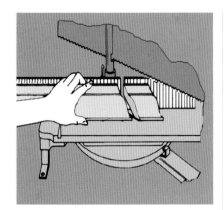 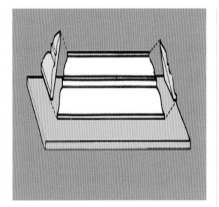 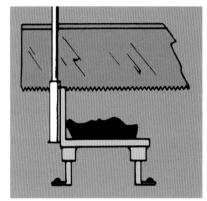

Step 1: Determine the length of the top shelf. Position the crown moulding front piece in a mitre box with the bottom of the moulding tightly against the fence. Set the saw angle at 45 degrees to left and slowly saw through the moulding.

Step 2: Carefully measure and cut the opposite end of the crown moulding front piece using the same technique but changing the mitre box angle exactly to 45 degrees to the right. Lay the moulding side piece in the mitre box and cut.

Step 3: The left and right end side piece angles are sawn using the same methods as employed when cutting the front piece angles. The right angled cuts are completed with the moulding lying flat on the saw bed and held tightly with the free hand.

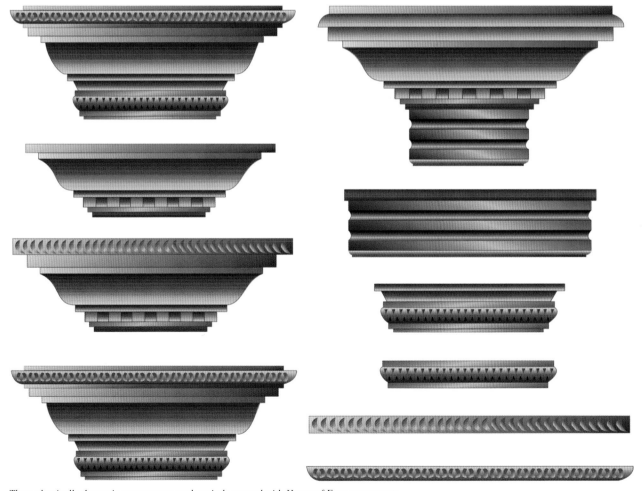

These classically dramatic crowns were each entirely created with House of Fara components.

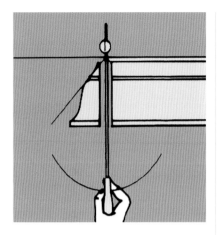

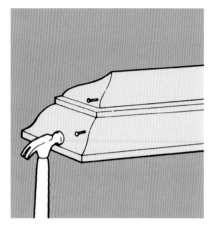

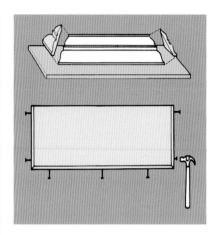

Step 4: The mitre saw is easily adjusted to create the right-angled and the 45-degree cuts. The two left and right end pieces have both types of angles. The front piece has the 45-degree angles cut into both ends.

Step 5: Assemble all pieces using stainable wood glue and finishing nails to create the complete crown moulding assembly. Countersink the nail heads and fill the holes with a matching wood putty.

Step 6: The crown moulding shelf is edge-finished with House of Fara strip mouldings. Fara offers several designs of embossed mouldings that can be glued to the edge of exposed lumber to create a carved look.

House of Fara offers both red oak and white oak mouldings in a large variety of high-quality and aesthetic designs.

Hardwood mantel constructed using off-the-shelf House of Fara hardwood mouldings.

Applique Mantel with Superior Fireplace Company High Efficiency Insert.

Master craftsman and designer Robert Wohners, Sr. combining the old and the new to create another masterpiece in wood.

Chapter Seven

The Custom Mantel

Commission a handcrafted mantel with today's master craftsmen.

As in the past you can still enjoy the thrill of partnering with master craftsmen like the Wohners family team to build the fireplace mantel of your dreams.

In the distant past, the fireplace mantel was the focal and gathering point for the entire clan. The aristocratic families would partner with master craftsmen to create and install a mantel that was unique for their home and that captured the love and dedication that the family felt toward their surroundings.

The Wohners family of master craftsmen and designers carries on this timeless tradition with skill and commitment. Their masterworks are a unique and personalized commission created and dedicated to family traditions.

The Wohners mantels created today obtain their inspiring great looks and tradition of workmanship from mantels made for the grand homes and palaces of the past.

Even though a knowledgeable carpenter can create a basic mantel, a truly classic mantel requires a professionally trained mantel designer partnering with a master wood carver and mantel

The Wohners family craftsmen created this timeless classic for an aristocratic setting.

builder. A carpenter uses standard lumberyard materials and moldings to create a mantel, along with mass produced ornaments which are applied to dress up the creation.

Professional designers and master craftsmen apply the aristocratic touch to custom mantels by specifying the finest hand-sorted hardwoods for the mantel core.

The mantel design is finalized through the application of the highest quality hand-carved ornamentation.

Ornaments come in a variety of materials. Each type of material has its benefits and drawbacks. The most utilized ornamental materials are carved wood, plaster or gesso, pressed (embossed) wood, and resin or plastic. As a rule carved wood is the best. It will last the longest, look the best and can be stained a

Wohners use sophisticated carving techniques to create their works of art in series. The ability to make multiple copies of a specific Wohner design keeps the final mantel cost in line for the customer.

variety of tones to blend with any mantel design or decor.

Resin or plastic is usually less expensive. However, oils from the casting process can cause painting failure over time and the material can become toxic if burned.

Pressed wood is a very shallow mock-carving technique and if painted the design can be hidden by the thickness of the paint.

Plaster becomes brittle over time and can crack because it does not expand and contract with the wood base on which it is applied.

Wohners uses solid or laminated wood for their applied ornaments almost exclusively.

With all ornamental materials the use of standard or series designs is the least costly. Dies, forms and machinery make duplication possible for a fraction

of the price of an original piece.

At Wohners these types of new designs are first drawn to scale and detailed before production. For larger projects where multiple copies are to be made for one customer a prototype is modeled in wood and or clay for the customer's approval.

When the entire mantelpiece is an original design that is more free form in design the ornamentation cannot be simply added onto the mantel. The entire design must be carved out of solid wood.

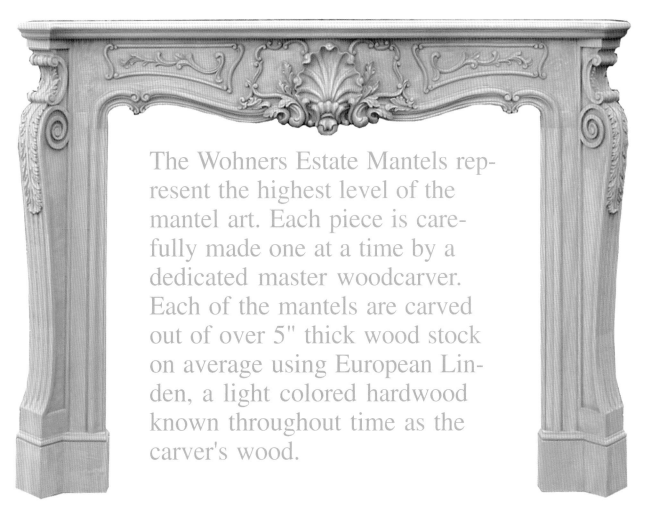

The Wohners Estate Mantels represent the highest level of the mantel art. Each piece is carefully made one at a time by a dedicated master woodcarver. Each of the mantels are carved out of over 5" thick wood stock on average using European Linden, a light colored hardwood known throughout time as the carver's wood.

For example, often the design bows out from the front as well as curving around the firebox. French Louis XIV and XV, Rococo and Renaissance revival styles are typically made this way.

The beauty of these designs comes from the organic flow of the line and the curve between ornaments. It requires a skilled wood sculptor to create this type of original mantel.

As with any art the execution is in the determination of its value and overall appearance. Beautifully executed pieces incorporate depth, undercut, shadow and line. It is important to convey to the artist the level of detail you would like on the piece at the beginning of the project. The craftsman then creates a masterpiece that directly reflects your original vision.

The Linden wood species was the favorite of Grinling Gibbons, the best and most famous woodcarver ever known.

Wohners applies the final finish carefully by hand to this elegant Estate Series carving.

350 years ago Grinling Gibbons was perfecting his craft. Today the Wohners are dedicated to preserving his time-honored traditions.

Gibbons was discovered by chance by the diarist John Evelyn from whom he was renting a cottage. "I saw the young man at his carving, by the light of a candle. I saw him to be engaged on a carved representation of Tintoretto's "Crucifixion", which he had in a frame of his own making".

Later that same evening he described what he had seen to Sir Christopher Wren. Christopher and Evelyn then introduced him to Charles II who gave him his first commission. It can still be seen in the dining room of Windsor Castle.

Of Gibbons, Horace Walpole wrote later,

"There is no instance of a man before Gibbons who gave wood the loose and airy lightness of flowers, and chained together the various productions of the elements with the free disorder natural to each species."

He was employed by Sir Christopher Wren to work on St. Paul's Cathedral and later was

This magnified view of Gibbon's work shows his dedication to natural detail.

appointed as master carver to George I. Many fine examples of his work can still be seen in the churches around London, particularly the choir stalls and organ case of St Paul's Cathedral.

Observers of the times said the Gibbon's carvings flowed like music. This example of his natural poetic style is still perfectly preserved.

Customers visit Wohners showroom to preview a wide selection of original mantels of traditional design.

Wohners' customers can select from a wide variety of finished mantels or create their own custom mantel from an exciting array of carvings. Selections include many highly styled classic mantel components.

Bob Wohners, Jr., "Shopping for a mantel can be a fun experience as you look to integrate the large variety of possible mantel designs into your home decor.

Wohners' customers can select from a wide variety of stock mantels or can customize their own. Depending on where you're located you can visit one of the country's largest mantel showrooms in New Jersey or if more convenient, you can visit Wohners website at www.wohners.com.

Arriving at the showroom you'll have the opportunity to preview a wide selection of original mantels in traditional designs. Wohners will greet you and spend time getting to know your personal design taste and home space requirements.

You'll learn about different size mantels and how to select the best size for your home. You'll explore Wohners' fine mantel detailing and craftsmanship and will view mantel designs that range from simple elegance to elaborate and ornate.

A simple mantel can be customized for your home by adding a variety of decorative carvings designed exclusively by Wohners. By mixing and matching a wide variety of existing components, a basic mantel can be transformed into an elegant masterpiece. At Wohners focusing on helping you to personalize you mantel results in a one-of-kind design uniquely your own."

Shopping for a mantel at Wohners is a lot of fun.

The Wohners showroom.
Customers visit the Wohners showroom to preview a wide selection of original mantels of traditional design.

A large variety of decorative carvings are offered.
A simple mantel can be customized by adding decorative carvings designed by Wohners. You'll choose from a wide variety of carvings when customizing your mantel.

Determining your personal design requirements.
Bob Wohners Jr. spends time getting to know the customer's personal design tastes and space requirements.

Choosing your basic mantel core.
The custom mantel begins with the selection of a correctly sized basic mantel that fits naturally with your space requirements.

Wohners' detailing and craftsmanship are legend.
Different sizes of mantels will be explained and you'll experience the fine detailing and exquisite craftsmanship of Wohners original mantel designs.

A point of interest mantel carving is chosen.
With the help of experts at Wohners, customers can mix and match components to change the look of a basic mantel.

Experience personal customer design consultations in the tradition of the old mantel masters. Wohners' one-on-one sessions ensure the highest quality of your mantel design and selection.

Wohners guides you through the mantel details.
The customer chooses a hand carved capital to be placed on the mantel column.

Working with a customer to design their personal mantel creation is a rewarding experience. Through hands on interactions, Wohners' customers review and select mantel components that appeal to their personal design and home decor preference. With guidance from a Wohners professional you can realize the mantel of your dreams and feel assured that you will receive expert advice.

Wohners brings the experience of over four generations of expert craftsmanship to each mantel design. Armed with these highly developed skills they can show you how to add elegance to your next custom mantel, whether you're looking for an ornate or classically elegant masterpiece.

Wohners and the customer finalize the custom mantel with the pre-assembly of individual components.

The mantel is mocked up for your approval.
The mantel cap is added to create a dramatic styling feature.
Design elements such as these signify a mantel masterpiece.

Hand-carved center pieces create a finishing touch.
The customer chooses a hand-carved centerpiece to be added
to her custom mantel at Wohners recommendation .

Wohners' craftsmen carefully hand assemble the mantel following the customer's classic design specs.

*Skilled craftsmen. Experienced craftsmen assemble the
final custom mantel.*

*Attention to detail. Four generations of experience in
building fine crafted mantels.*

*Quality sturdy construction. High-quality screw bolt
connectors firmly assemble the mantel components.*

*Carved solid wood appliques. A large selection of
masterfully carved mantel carved accents are always
available.*

Elegant estate paneling. Precision assembled hardwood over panels are available to meet any styling requirements.

Heirloom crowning touches. Wohners' craftsmen add the final touches to the customer's well-styled mantel emsemble.

The customer's finished mantel has the timeless integrity of the Renaissance master builders.

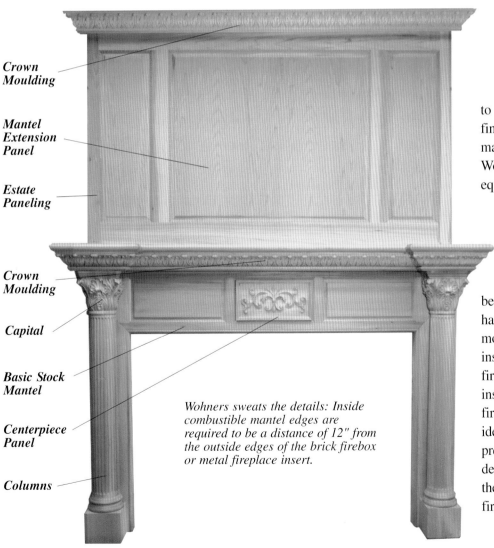

Crown Moulding

Mantel Extension Panel

Estate Paneling

Crown Moulding

Capital

Basic Stock Mantel

Centerpiece Panel

Columns

Wohners sweats the details: Inside combustible mantel edges are required to be a distance of 12" from the outside edges of the brick firebox or metal fireplace insert.

The careful attention to detail is reflected in the final version of the mantel assembled by Wohners in their well-equipped workshop.

Wohners mantels can be modified to fit both hand-laid brick and the modern steel fireplace inserts. Also, numerous fireplace mantels are installed with faux fireplace inserts. This is ideal when the client prefers the classic mantel decorating theme without the actual working firebox installation.

Wohners crafstmen carve a complete universe of highly detailed and well-researched hand-carved appliques.

Just like the Old Masters, Wohners craftsmen apply time-honored step-by-step wood carving techniques.

1. Pattern is transferred to wood. The carving wood is loosely glued to a back up wood that is later removed for shaping the final outside profile.

2. Pattern is hogged out with a large tipped power tool. The craftsman stays outside the lines to rough out the basic shape of the sketched design.

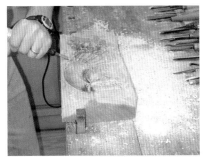

3. Design is further detailed with a smaller tip in the power tool. The sculpting is tightened up prior to fine detailing with multiple hand tools.

4. Refining the overall shape. A bandsaw is used to remove excess material from the outside outline. The saw stays 1/8" outside the outline.

5. Hand-carving the finest details. Carving gouges, v-tools and other hand tools bring out the beauty and texture of the artist's original drawing.

6. Protective finishes highlight the beauty. Each job requires specific applications of finishes to fit the client's decor and the mantel's environment.

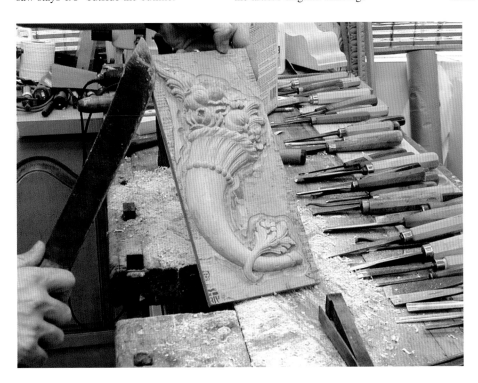

7. Final carving touches are completed. The refined carving is finished by routing out the precise outline surrounding the design.

To accomplish this the carving is first temporarily attached to a disposable backing board.

The backing board acts as a clamp base for the delicate carving details applied with a high speed hand router.

The hand carved applique is now ready for attachment to the base mantel.

*8. **Panels are hand routed.*** All straight line machine cuts are carefully crafted by hand using a power router adding depth and beauty to the final application.

*9. **Attaching hand-carved detailing.*** With high quality glue, power nailers and screw guns, all final details are attached to the mantel parts.

*10. **Centerpiece is guided into place.*** The final carved mantel centerpiece is positioned into the mantel center panel with an emphasis on flawlessness.

*11. **Final appliques complete the mantel.*** Craftsmen attach beautifully crafted appliques with precision to the final mantel.

The final assembled Wohners mantel reflects Renaissance design beauty and will become a timeless heirloom for future generations.

The customer's final Wohners mantel is caulked and painted to match the home decor. It will be a treasure to enjoy for generations to come.

Things for you to consider when you plan your fireplace and mantel design and installation.

Fireplace Location

When selecting a location it is important to evaluate a number of considerations. Modern construction techniques can create conditions that may not allow your chimney to draft properly. This may result in smoke spillage from your fireplace, as well as cause other combustion appliances to operate incorrectly.

Sealing Construction

Tightly sealed construction is important for energy efficiency. A great deal of effort has been directed to tightening up sidewall construction, while less attention has been paid to tightening upper portions of the warm air envelope (insulated ceilings).

The Stack Effect

This has increased the "Stack Effect", a condition that increases the negative pressure generated by the structure. This negative pressure affects the performance of a fireplace chimney. To minimize the negative pressure generated by stack effect make certain that all ductwork installed in the attic spaces is airtight.

Minimize Light Fixtures

Minimize the number of recessed light fixtures installed in the insulated ceiling, and use sealed recessed light fixtures.

Sealed Accessories

Make certain the whole house fans and attic access panels are tightly sealed. These are important design considerations that must be observed during the design and construction stage of the home.

Basement Fireplaces

If you desire to put a fireplace in your basement, we recommend that you consider a direct vent gas fireplace.

Cold Flue Backdrafting

Basements have negative air pressure that causes the fireplace system to be susceptible to smoke spillage and cold flue backdrafting.

Since direct vent gas fireplaces are sealed they are not affected by the negative pressure.

Chimney Location

Finally, woodburning fireplaces perform best when their chimney (roof termination) is located on the upper half of the roof, especially when cathedral ceilings are present.

Lazy Flues

Chimneys that are located on the lower half of the roof realize what is known as "lazy flue" and will not draft as well as a chimney that is located in the upper portion of the roof. The reason for this is that the stack effect generated by the overall height of the living spaces inside the house will exceed the draft generated by the chimney system.

Termination Caps

If you desire to place a woodburning fireplace in a location where the termination cap would be located on the lower half of a roof, such as on an outside wall at the base of a cathedral ceiling, we recommend that you consider using a direct vent gas fireplace. This will assure the homeowner a fireplace that operates correctly.

> **The various subjects we've discussed here do not affect just your woodburning factory-built fireplace. They can cause any woodburning fireplace as well as any conventionally vented (B-vent) gas appliance to operate improperly. Careful planning at this stage of your project will ensure satisfaction with the operation of your fireplace once it is completed.**
>
> *- Heat N' Glo*

Woodcarver Greg Young carves ruggedly beautiful mantels from ancient timbers he salvages from old Wisconsin barns.

Chapter Eight

The Rustic Mantel

Nature's beauty is displayed in Greg Young's carved mantels.

Greg shows us step by step how he creates keepsake mantels from weathered old barn wood beams. His folksy designs are crafted with the warmth of backwoods Wisconsin friendliness.

The county seat town where I grew up was in the heartland of west central Indiana. It was prime farm country, which meant that there were barns, most of them already old, dotting the landscape.

Although I didn't grow up on a farm, I learned to drive a tractor, bail hail, and put up hay in the barn hay loft to make money at summer jobs while I was in high school.

Whenever I walked into a cavernous old barn I was always awestruck by it's size, in particular the size of the hand-hewn timbers that spanned the barn's interior. From the massive size of the timbers, to my youthful mind, those barns would stand forever. But now that I'm older I have sadly come to realize that these massive old barns, symbols of permanence and our agrarian heritage, were vulnerable.

Over the years our old barns have started to disappear from our rural landscape. One doesn't have to drive far to see once tall, proud old barns falling into states of disrepair, and eventually collapsing.

But just as the grand old barns are vanishing, there are those people who have come to realize the value and inherent beauty of the old wood in those barns, and who have found new uses for that old weathered wood, reclaiming some of the rich rural heritage that is our past. That old wood recovered is now generally referred to as reclaimed timber.

Whenever I walked into a cavernous old barn I was always awestruck by the size of the hand-hewn timbers that spanned the barn's interior.

Greg's rustic carvings add a woodsy style and feel to his mantel creations.

There are numerous reasons that I was drawn to carving fireplace mantels out of old barn timbers. For one, working with this old wood has provided a way for me to revisit my history and heritage of growing up in Indiana farm country.

Many of the barn timbers that I work with were hand hewn and several decades old. I also like to work with these old timbers because of the character they possess. They have been tempered and tested by the years and the elements, all of which have forged a gorgeous patina that one rarely, if ever, finds in new timber.

Because the early farmers regularly made their barns out of timber that was readily available, you will find barn timbers fashioned from a wide array of species of timber. Those I carved for this project happen to be pine, but I have come across barn beams fashioned out of hickory, oak, maple, butternut, pine, and even walnut. In certain parts of the country, Douglas Fir was a popular choice.

Whatever the wood, if you undertake carving an old barn beam, you will be challenged and amazed at the beauty of the wood which lies just beneath the old marred surface. In fact, in discovering the beauty of that old wood, you may find yourself saying what I have said on more than one occasion while carving the wood, "You just can't find beautiful timber like that anymore!"

Greg uses a personal set of carving tools that he has perfected over his many years of crafting keepsakes.

Because of the rather brittle nature of the old pine timbers that Greg works with for his projects he uses a wide variety of woodworking tools including professional quality power tools and hand tools. Here's a list of the tools Greg has found to be most useful:

10mm #7 palm gouge

Roto Zip with both 1/4 and 1/8 inch collets and plunge router attachment and various bits.

Bench knife

1/8" - 3/8" v-tools

#3 sweep 20mm carving gouge

Foredom rotary power carver and various burrs and bits.

Greg walks us through his carefully crafted process of carving the rustic mantel with basic tools.

1. Select your mantel timber.

Select the most unmarred side of the barn timber for the face of the mantel. In choosing the face, you'll want to present the mantel so that the most marred side will be put up against the hearth.

The timber pictured has cracks running horizontally with the wood grain. Unless the cracks remind you vaguely of the grand canyon they shouldn't pose much of a problem in carving the mantel.

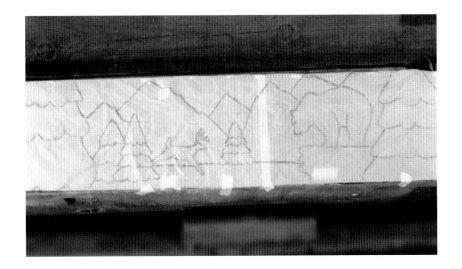

2. Prep your mantel timber.

To prepare the mantel face and sides for carving you'll first want to remove as much grit and grime as possible so that your carving tools won't be damaged. A power drill with a wire brush works well to clean up the timber. In using a wire brush, be sure to wear eye protection and a good dust filter mask.

3. Layout your carving pattern.

In laying out a pattern, first find the center point of the mantel face. This mantel is 76" long, 8" wide by 8" tall. Use tracing paper to lay out the scene or design. Center the scene, then carefully place carbon paper under the length of the scene. Use a pencil to trace the pattern onto the mantel face. Greg prefers to design a scene that can be centered in the mantel face.

4. *Preview your pattern.*

Remove the tracing and carbon paper to preview your transferred pattern. Your tracing should be clearly legible when you begin to carve.

5. *Establish your stop cuts.*

Darken the area on the mantel scene that will be carved deepest. This scene will be high relief carved to a maximum depth of about 2".

Establish stop cuts and depth by using a Roto Zip with a 1/8" spiral cutting bit. Here Greg is using the plunge router attachment. When using the spiral and plunge router bits be sure to not cut deeper than 1/4" increments, increasing the depth with each pass until the desired depth is achieved.

6. *Establish the different depth levels in your carving.*

Having established stop cuts Greg begins to establish the different depth levels by using a 1/2" fluted plunge router bit.

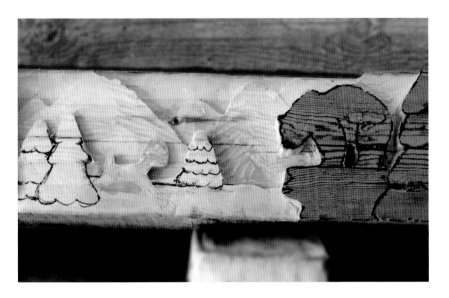

7. *Result.*

There are six different levels of depth to this carving scene. The closest objects have the greatest depth. The trees framing the scene are 1" deep. The further into the scene the greater the compression of the objects. The remaining levels average 1/4" deep. The sky is carved 1/2" deeper than the mountains. Also Greg has made another copy of the deer and using a spray adhesive applied it to the scene.

8. *Use the Foredom to define your scene.*

Switching to the Foredom carefully create a stop cut around the deer defining it by using a #113 Dremel pencil grinder bit. Continue to use this bit to define the other objects in the scene as well.

9. *Superglue preserves the more intricate parts of your carving.*

Yes, it's super glue. In working with this old pine, one of the challenges is it's brittleness. So before carving more and undercutting the objects first saturate the most fragile parts in a thin layer of super glue. In this particular pattern the primary concern is the deer's antlers.

10. Undercut the prominent objects in your scene.

After defining the objects throughout the scene put a 1/8" roto zip spiral saw bit into the Foredom handpiece and begin to carefully undercut the more prominent objects in the foreground. Please note: Be careful not to carve deeper than the scene behind the object that you are undercutting.

11. Refine the undercuts.

In addition to undercutting with the spiral saw bit use a #3, 20mm gouge to refine the undercutting. In undercutting the objects in the scene that are only 1/4" deep or less carefully undercut the objects using a #113 Dremel pencil grinder in the Foredom hand piece.

12. Examine the results of your undercuts.

Notice how the undercutting gives dimension and depth to the scene.

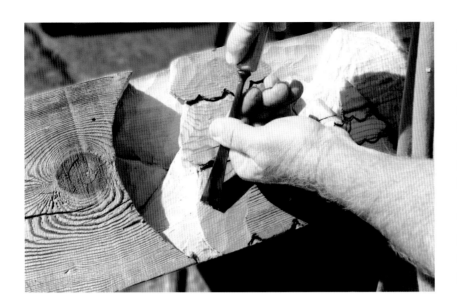

13. *Shape and define the objects in your scene.*

Using the #3, 20mm gouge begin to round and shape the larger objects, shaping and defining the trees and mountains. For the smaller trees and background mountains use a #7, 10mm gouge to get in tighter places.

To shape the bear and deer use the Foredom rotary carver utilizing medium and small flame shaped ruby carving burrs.

14. *Use your v-tools to add texture.*

For this mantel scene Greg is using a 3/8" v-tool to texture the trees. On the smaller background trees he uses a 1/8" v-tool to texture them.

15. *Use your Foredom to add fur-like texture.*

To texture the fur of the bear and deer use your Foredom. Greg prefers using a very small flame tipped diamond stone to create a nice fur texture.

16. Stamping techniques for added depth.

Greg likes to stamp the sky, the deepest background in the mantel. This techinique will give the effect of added depth. Stamping breaks up the reflective surface of the wood, thereby creating an illusion of depth.

Greg creates his own personal stamping tools by deeply cross-etching the flat top of a bolt and large nail with a triangular metal file.

17. Use a hammer with your stamp tool.

Use a hammer with your stamping tool to carefully stamp the background. You can create charming depth and texture with this technique.

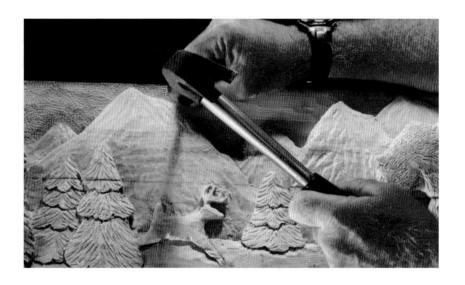

18. Result of using stamp tools.

As this picture shows, Greg's skillful use of hand fabricated stamp tools adds an unique and woodsy touch to his original mantels.

19. Stamping techniques for added depth.

Except for cleaning up any areas of the scene that might have errant tags of wood left over from the carving, this mantel is ready to seal.

20. Seal your mantel creation. Use a fast drying sanding sealer to seal the mantel.

I took up woodcarving because I've always enjoyed working with wood, and I have found the art of wood-carving to be therapeutic, a very nice counterpoint to working with people.

Greg Young

You can read more about Greg and his unique wood carvings and custom mantels by visiting his website at www.gregyoungcarvings.com.

Greg Young Gallery

I. Bird of Prey

II. Ocean View

III. Creation

IV. Northern Exposure

V. Bear Necessity

VI. Playful Friends

VII. Mighty Bison

VIII. Stream Scene

Cherrywood Fireplace Mantel with Superior Fireplace Company refractory brick and steel fireplace.

Chapter Nine

Mantels Portfolio

Exploded Views and Illustrations of Original Designs

Mantel planning and design is easy using these informative overviews. Suggested materials are readily available at most lumber yards at affordable prices. Parts are shaped with common tools. The designs are easily completed in your spare time.

Important design note: When planning your original fireplace mantel design, carefully coordinate the style of the mantel you design and build with the type of firebox you fit it with. The zero-clearance gas and wood fireplaces allow the mantel to fit right against the firebox opening. Standard steel open-fire fireplaces and the classic brick and mortar units must be allowed clearance for combustible materials. On standard fireplaces that translates to at least six inches of space between the firebox front edge and the combustible mantel materials that fit close to it.

Laguna, pg. 90

Woodside, pg. 91

Sherwood, pg. 92

Cherrybeane, pg. 93

Cherrywood, pg. 94

Oak Manor, pg. 95

Mohawk, pg. 96

Cherrytree, pg. 97

Temple, pg. 98

Timberview, pg. 99

Fawn Manor, pg. 100

Palacian, pg. 101

Celecia, pg. 102

Pharoah, pg. 103

Psychodelic, pg. 104

Afrikan, pg. 105

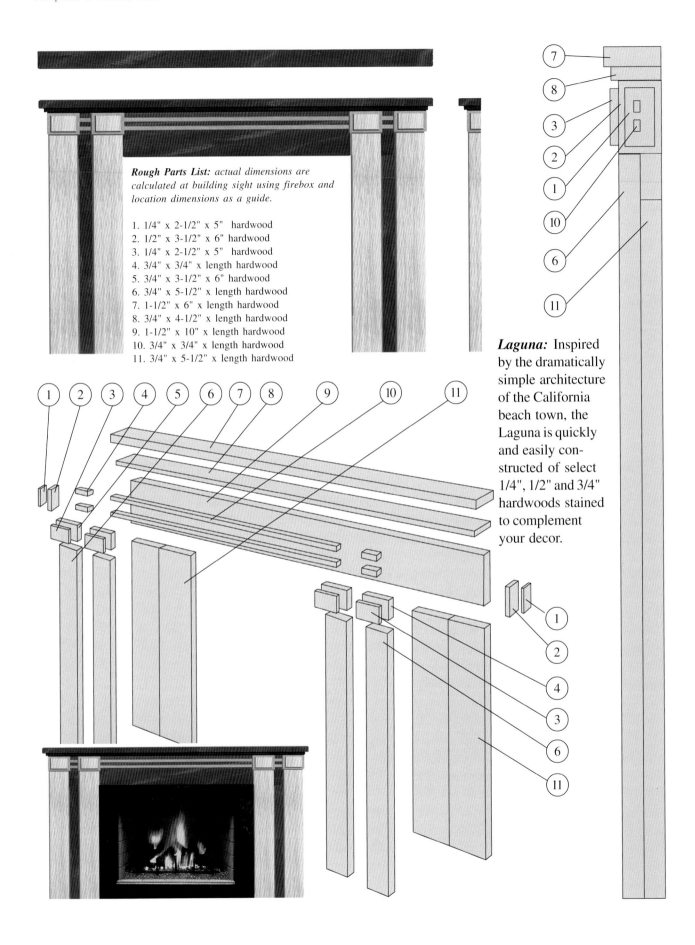

Rough Parts List: *actual dimensions are calculated at building sight using firebox and location dimensions as a guide.*

1. 1/4" x 2-1/2" x 5" hardwood
2. 1/2" x 3-1/2" x 6" hardwood
3. 1/4" x 2-1/2" x 5" hardwood
4. 3/4" x 3/4" x length hardwood
5. 3/4" x 3-1/2" x 6" hardwood
6. 3/4" x 5-1/2" x length hardwood
7. 1-1/2" x 6" x length hardwood
8. 3/4" x 4-1/2" x length hardwood
9. 1-1/2" x 10" x length hardwood
10. 3/4" x 3/4" x length hardwood
11. 3/4" x 5-1/2" x length hardwood

Laguna: Inspired by the dramatically simple architecture of the California beach town, the Laguna is quickly and easily constructed of select 1/4", 1/2" and 3/4" hardwoods stained to complement your decor.

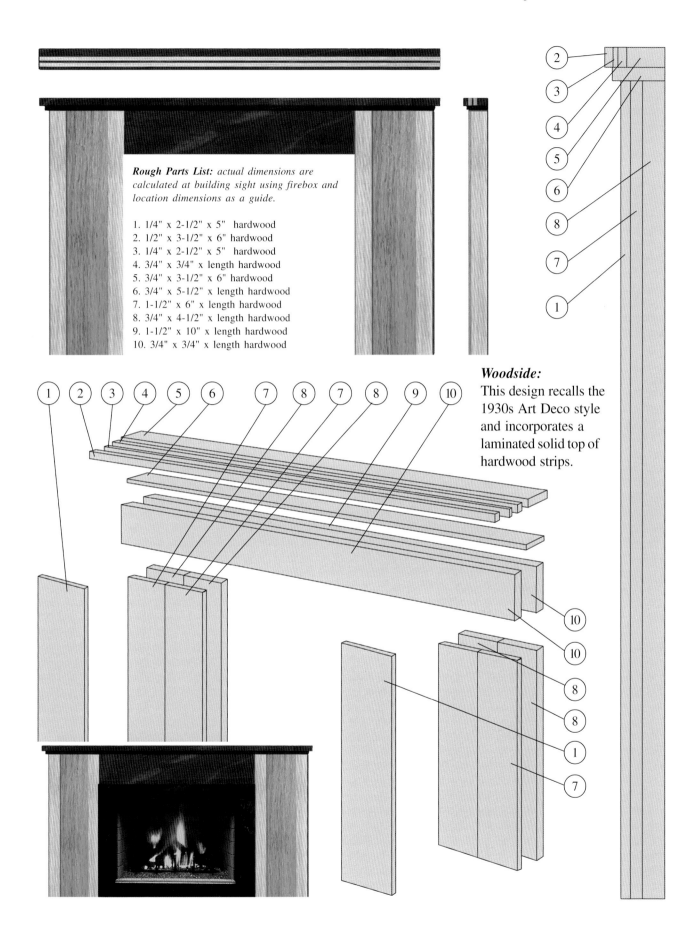

Rough Parts List: *actual dimensions are calculated at building sight using firebox and location dimensions as a guide.*

1. 1/4" x 2-1/2" x 5" hardwood
2. 1/2" x 3-1/2" x 6" hardwood
3. 1/4" x 2-1/2" x 5" hardwood
4. 3/4" x 3/4" x length hardwood
5. 3/4" x 3-1/2" x 6" hardwood
6. 3/4" x 5-1/2" x length hardwood
7. 1-1/2" x 6" x length hardwood
8. 3/4" x 4-1/2" x length hardwood
9. 1-1/2" x 10" x length hardwood
10. 3/4" x 3/4" x length hardwood

Woodside:

This design recalls the 1930s Art Deco style and incorporates a laminated solid top of hardwood strips.

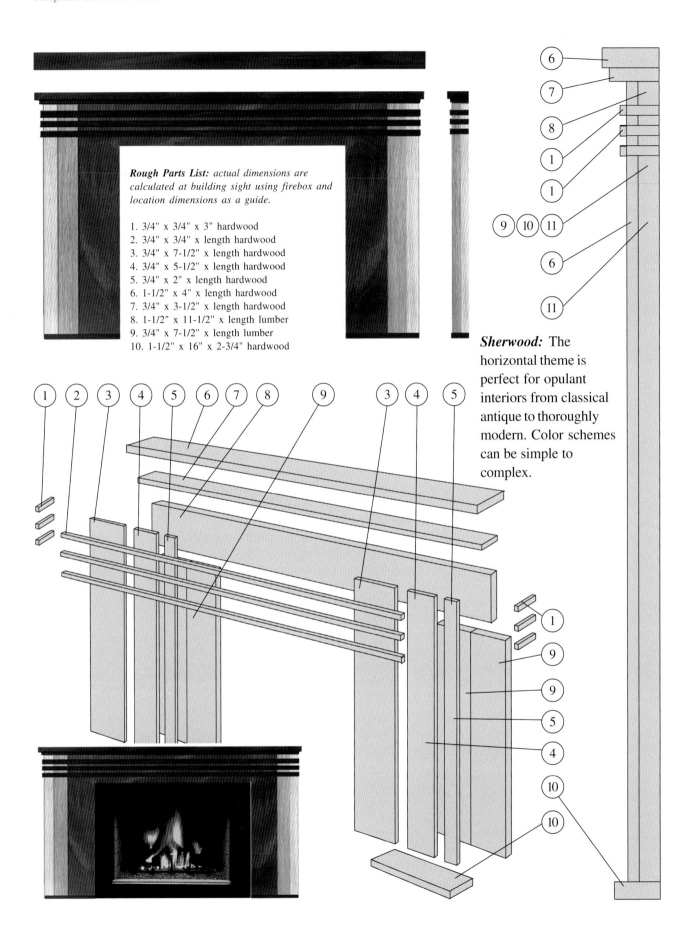

Rough Parts List: *actual dimensions are calculated at building sight using firebox and location dimensions as a guide.*

1. 3/4" x 3/4" x 3" hardwood
2. 3/4" x 3/4" x length hardwood
3. 3/4" x 7-1/2" x length hardwood
4. 3/4" x 5-1/2" x length hardwood
5. 3/4" x 2" x length hardwood
6. 1-1/2" x 4" x length hardwood
7. 3/4" x 3-1/2" x length hardwood
8. 1-1/2" x 11-1/2" x length lumber
9. 3/4" x 7-1/2" x length lumber
10. 1-1/2" x 16" x 2-3/4" hardwood

Sherwood: The horizontal theme is perfect for opulant interiors from classical antique to thoroughly modern. Color schemes can be simple to complex.

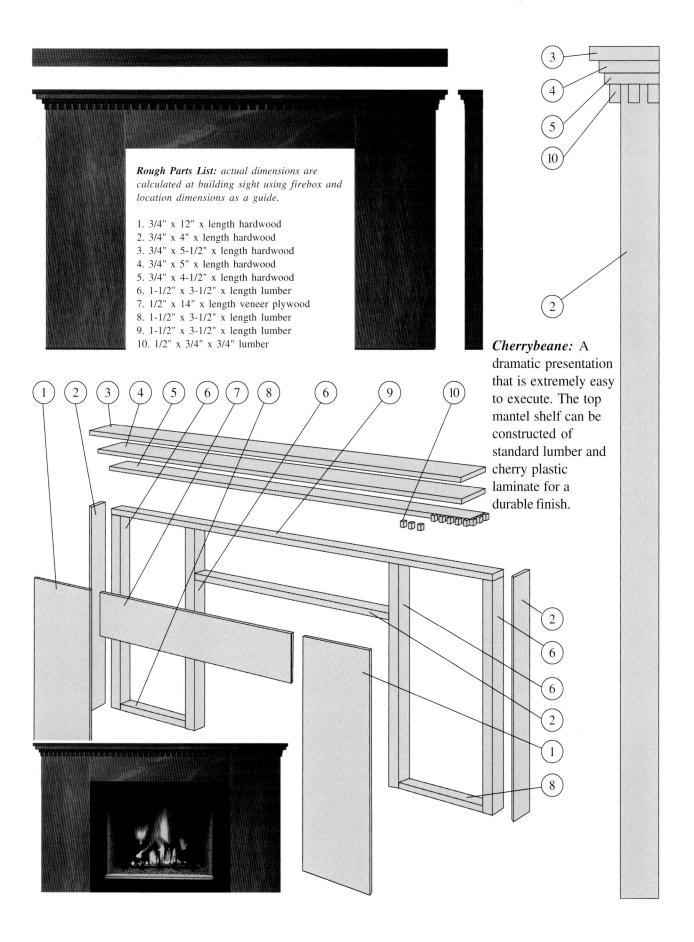

Rough Parts List: *actual dimensions are calculated at building sight using firebox and location dimensions as a guide.*

1. 3/4" x 12" x length hardwood
2. 3/4" x 4" x length hardwood
3. 3/4" x 5-1/2" x length hardwood
4. 3/4" x 5" x length hardwood
5. 3/4" x 4-1/2" x length hardwood
6. 1-1/2" x 3-1/2" x length lumber
7. 1/2" x 14" x length veneer plywood
8. 1-1/2" x 3-1/2" x length lumber
9. 1-1/2" x 3-1/2" x length lumber
10. 1/2" x 3/4" x 3/4" lumber

Cherrybeane: A dramatic presentation that is extremely easy to execute. The top mantel shelf can be constructed of standard lumber and cherry plastic laminate for a durable finish.

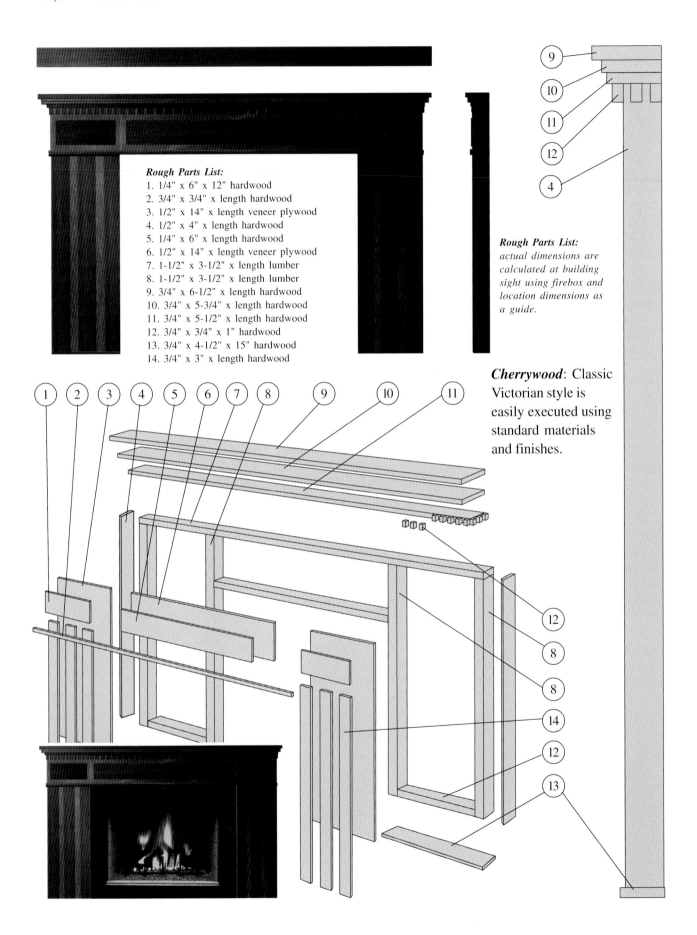

Rough Parts List:
1. 1/4" x 6" x 12" hardwood
2. 3/4" x 3/4" x length hardwood
3. 1/2" x 14" x length veneer plywood
4. 1/2" x 4" x length hardwood
5. 1/4" x 6" x length hardwood
6. 1/2" x 14" x length veneer plywood
7. 1-1/2" x 3-1/2" x length lumber
8. 1-1/2" x 3-1/2" x length lumber
9. 3/4" x 6-1/2" x length hardwood
10. 3/4" x 5-3/4" x length hardwood
11. 3/4" x 5-1/2" x length hardwood
12. 3/4" x 3/4" x 1" hardwood
13. 3/4" x 4-1/2" x 15" hardwood
14. 3/4" x 3" x length hardwood

Rough Parts List:
actual dimensions are calculated at building sight using firebox and location dimensions as a guide.

Cherrywood: Classic Victorian style is easily executed using standard materials and finishes.

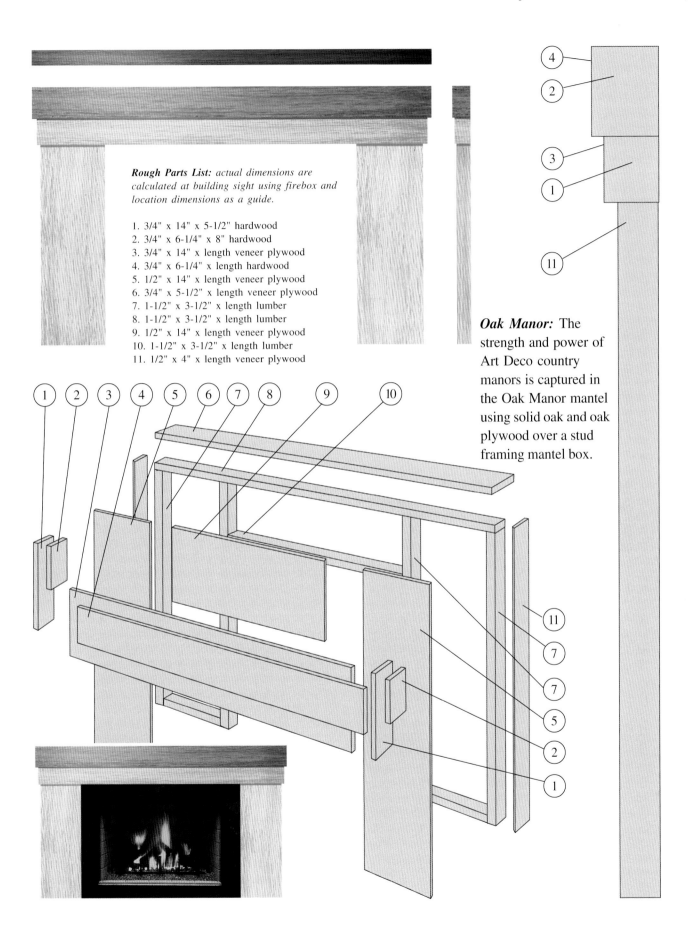

Rough Parts List: *actual dimensions are calculated at building sight using firebox and location dimensions as a guide.*

1. 3/4" x 14" x 5-1/2" hardwood
2. 3/4" x 6-1/4" x 8" hardwood
3. 3/4" x 14" x length veneer plywood
4. 3/4" x 6-1/4" x length hardwood
5. 1/2" x 14" x length veneer plywood
6. 3/4" x 5-1/2" x length veneer plywood
7. 1-1/2" x 3-1/2" x length lumber
8. 1-1/2" x 3-1/2" x length lumber
9. 1/2" x 14" x length veneer plywood
10. 1-1/2" x 3-1/2" x length lumber
11. 1/2" x 4" x length veneer plywood

Oak Manor: The strength and power of Art Deco country manors is captured in the Oak Manor mantel using solid oak and oak plywood over a stud framing mantel box.

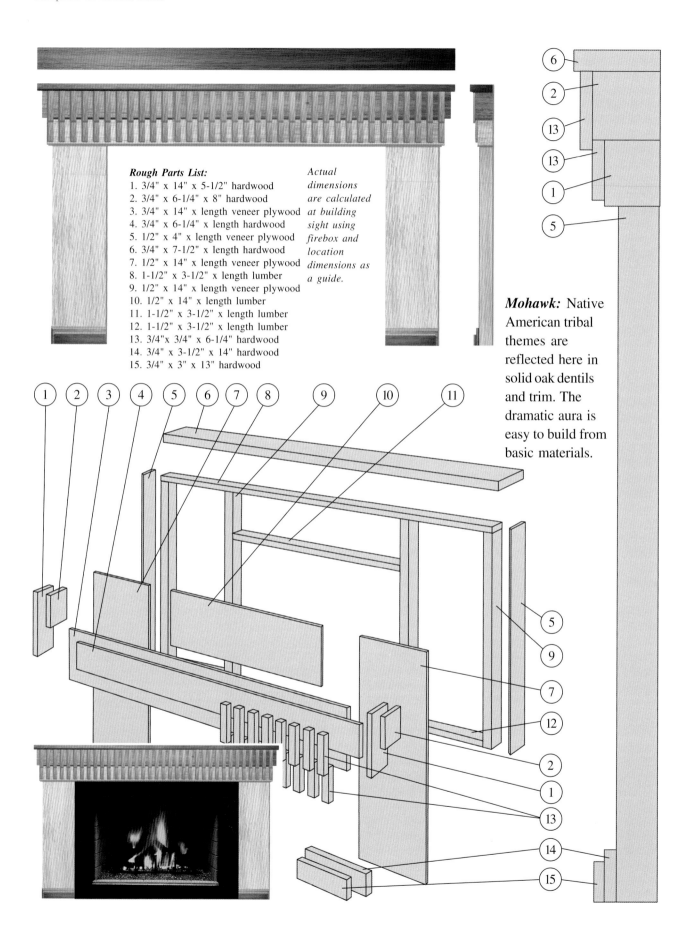

Rough Parts List:
1. 3/4" x 14" x 5-1/2" hardwood
2. 3/4" x 6-1/4" x 8" hardwood
3. 3/4" x 14" x length veneer plywood
4. 3/4" x 6-1/4" x length hardwood
5. 1/2" x 4" x length veneer plywood
6. 3/4" x 7-1/2" x length hardwood
7. 1/2" x 14" x length veneer plywood
8. 1-1/2" x 3-1/2" x length lumber
9. 1/2" x 14" x length veneer plywood
10. 1/2" x 14" x length lumber
11. 1-1/2" x 3-1/2" x length lumber
12. 1-1/2" x 3-1/2" x length lumber
13. 3/4"x 3/4" x 6-1/4" hardwood
14. 3/4" x 3-1/2" x 14" hardwood
15. 3/4" x 3" x 13" hardwood

Actual dimensions are calculated at building sight using firebox and location dimensions as a guide.

Mohawk: Native American tribal themes are reflected here in solid oak dentils and trim. The dramatic aura is easy to build from basic materials.

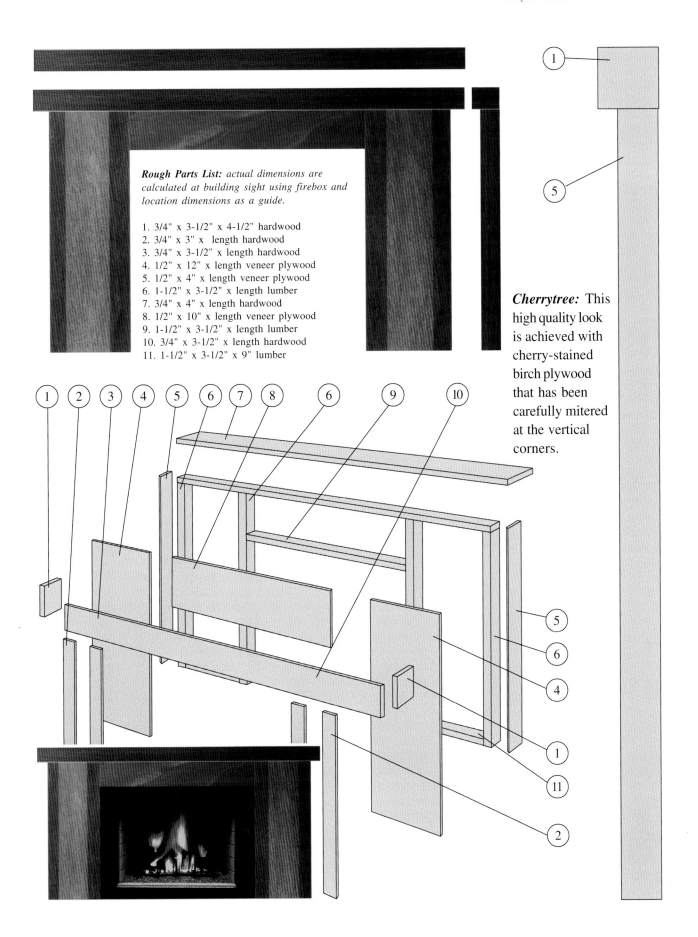

Rough Parts List: *actual dimensions are calculated at building sight using firebox and location dimensions as a guide.*

1. 3/4" x 3-1/2" x 4-1/2" hardwood
2. 3/4" x 3" x length hardwood
3. 3/4" x 3-1/2" x length hardwood
4. 1/2" x 12" x length veneer plywood
5. 1/2" x 4" x length veneer plywood
6. 1-1/2" x 3-1/2" x length lumber
7. 3/4" x 4" x length hardwood
8. 1/2" x 10" x length veneer plywood
9. 1-1/2" x 3-1/2" x length lumber
10. 3/4" x 3-1/2" x length hardwood
11. 1-1/2" x 3-1/2" x 9" lumber

Cherrytree: This high quality look is achieved with cherry-stained birch plywood that has been carefully mitered at the vertical corners.

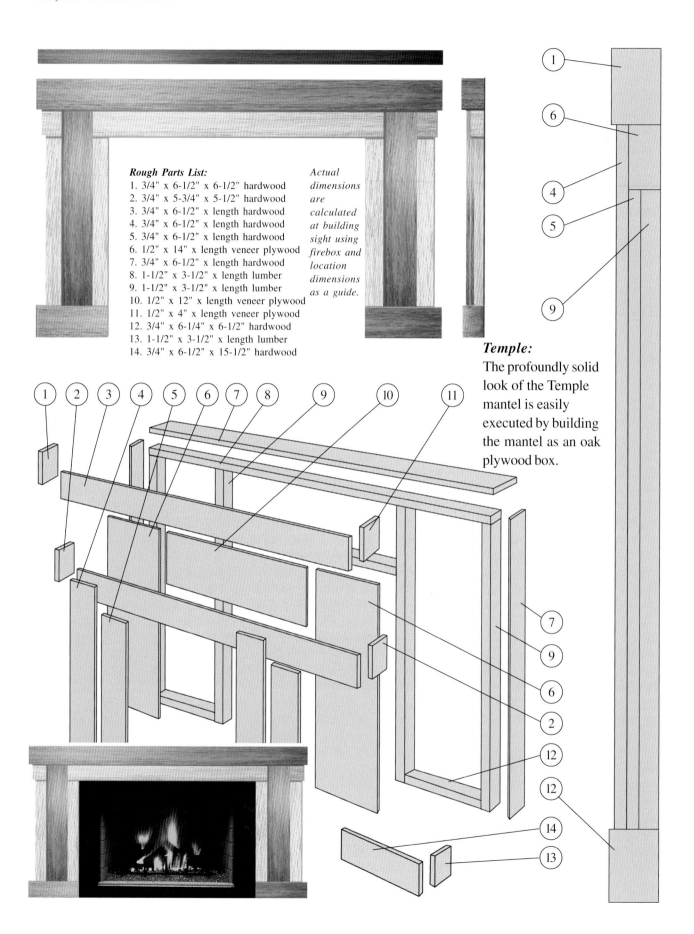

Rough Parts List:
1. 3/4" x 6-1/2" x 6-1/2" hardwood
2. 3/4" x 5-3/4" x 5-1/2" hardwood
3. 3/4" x 6-1/2" x length hardwood
4. 3/4" x 6-1/2" x length hardwood
5. 3/4" x 6-1/2" x length hardwood
6. 1/2" x 14" x length veneer plywood
7. 3/4" x 6-1/2" x length hardwood
8. 1-1/2" x 3-1/2" x length lumber
9. 1-1/2" x 3-1/2" x length lumber
10. 1/2" x 12" x length veneer plywood
11. 1/2" x 4" x length veneer plywood
12. 3/4" x 6-1/4" x 6-1/2" hardwood
13. 1-1/2" x 3-1/2" x length lumber
14. 3/4" x 6-1/2" x 15-1/2" hardwood

Actual dimensions are calculated at building sight using firebox and location dimensions as a guide.

Temple:
The profoundly solid look of the Temple mantel is easily executed by building the mantel as an oak plywood box.

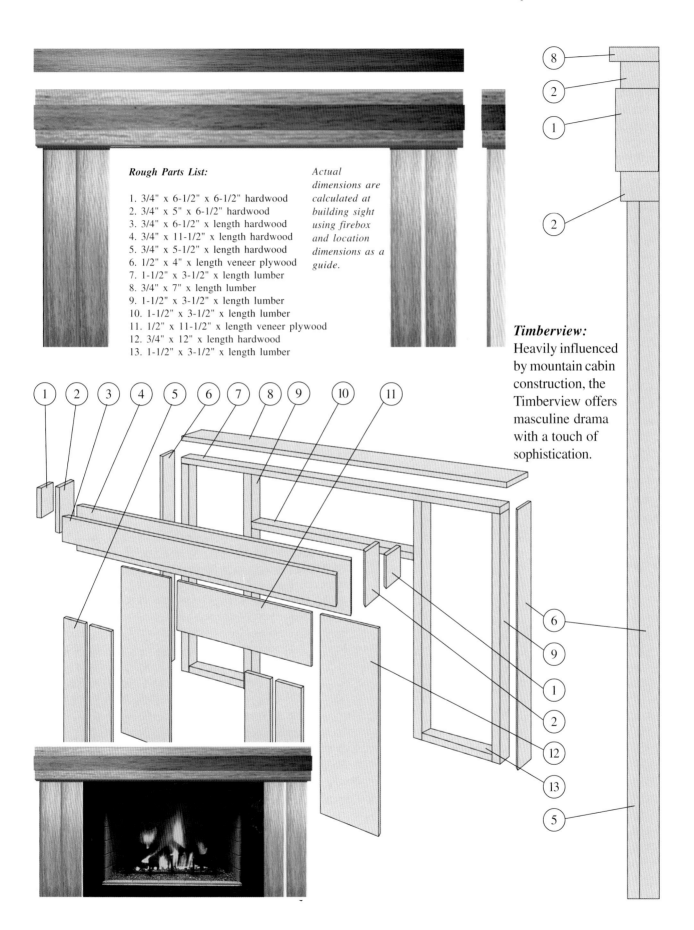

Rough Parts List:

1. 3/4" x 6-1/2" x 6-1/2" hardwood
2. 3/4" x 5" x 6-1/2" hardwood
3. 3/4" x 6-1/2" x length hardwood
4. 3/4" x 11-1/2" x length hardwood
5. 3/4" x 5-1/2" x length hardwood
6. 1/2" x 4" x length veneer plywood
7. 1-1/2" x 3-1/2" x length lumber
8. 3/4" x 7" x length lumber
9. 1-1/2" x 3-1/2" x length lumber
10. 1-1/2" x 3-1/2" x length lumber
11. 1/2" x 11-1/2" x length veneer plywood
12. 3/4" x 12" x length hardwood
13. 1-1/2" x 3-1/2" x length lumber

Actual dimensions are calculated at building sight using firebox and location dimensions as a guide.

Timberview:
Heavily influenced by mountain cabin construction, the Timberview offers masculine drama with a touch of sophistication.

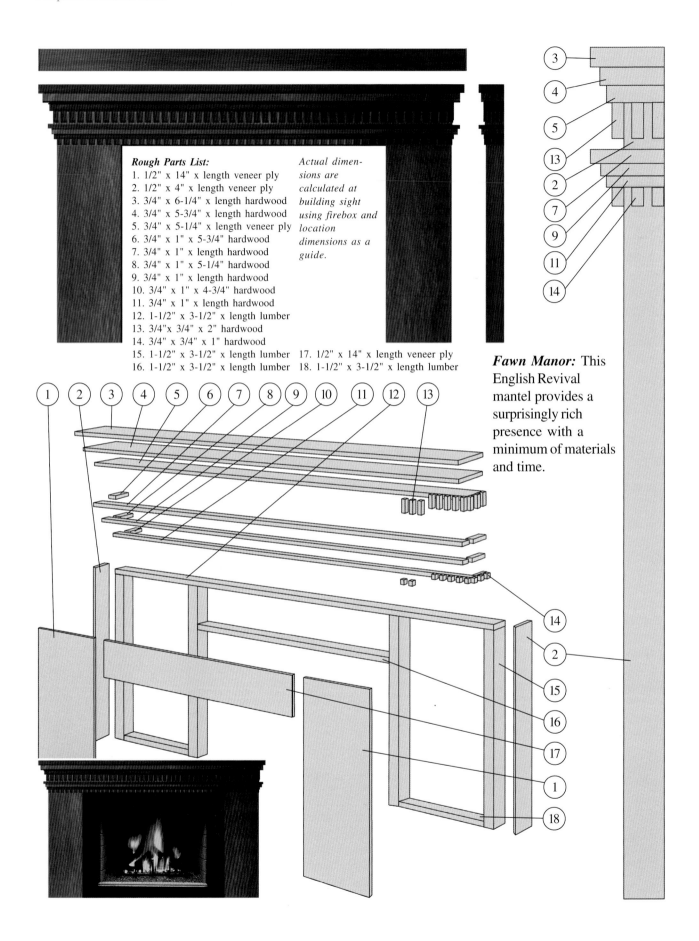

Rough Parts List:
1. 1/2" x 14" x length veneer ply
2. 1/2" x 4" x length veneer ply
3. 3/4" x 6-1/4" x length hardwood
4. 3/4" x 5-3/4" x length hardwood
5. 3/4" x 5-1/4" x length veneer ply
6. 3/4" x 1" x 5-3/4" hardwood
7. 3/4" x 1" x length hardwood
8. 3/4" x 1" x 5-1/4" hardwood
9. 3/4" x 1" x length hardwood
10. 3/4" x 1" x 4-3/4" hardwood
11. 3/4" x 1" x length hardwood
12. 1-1/2" x 3-1/2" x length lumber
13. 3/4"x 3/4" x 2" hardwood
14. 3/4" x 3/4" x 1" hardwood
15. 1-1/2" x 3-1/2" x length lumber
16. 1-1/2" x 3-1/2" x length lumber
17. 1/2" x 14" x length veneer ply
18. 1-1/2" x 3-1/2" x length lumber

Actual dimensions are calculated at building sight using firebox and location dimensions as a guide.

Fawn Manor: This English Revival mantel provides a surprisingly rich presence with a minimum of materials and time.

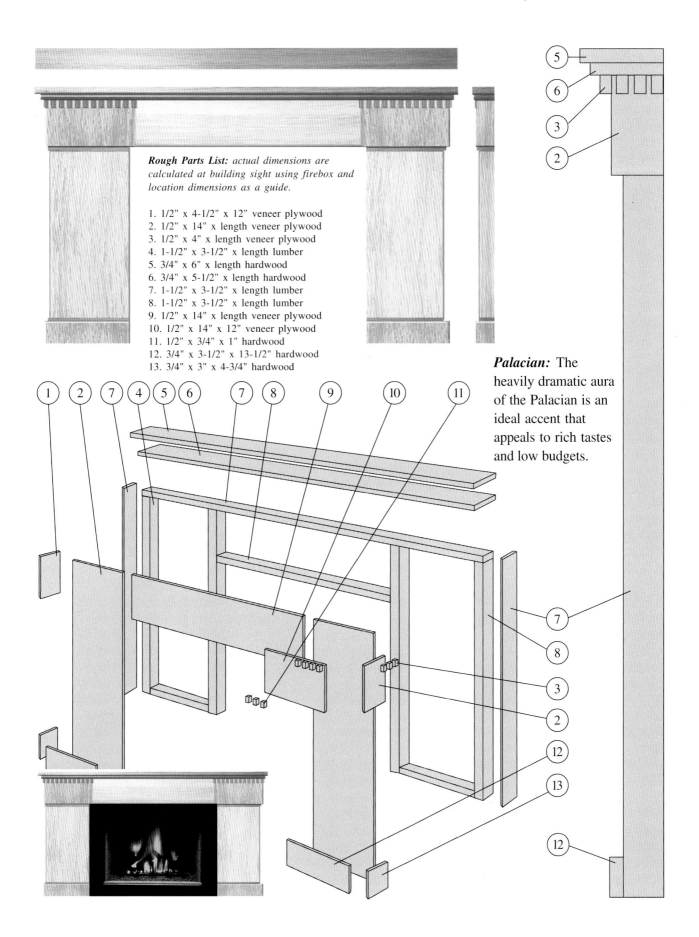

Rough Parts List: *actual dimensions are calculated at building sight using firebox and location dimensions as a guide.*

1. 1/2" x 4-1/2" x 12" veneer plywood
2. 1/2" x 14" x length veneer plywood
3. 1/2" x 4" x length veneer plywood
4. 1-1/2" x 3-1/2" x length lumber
5. 3/4" x 6" x length hardwood
6. 3/4" x 5-1/2" x length hardwood
7. 1-1/2" x 3-1/2" x length lumber
8. 1-1/2" x 3-1/2" x length lumber
9. 1/2" x 14" x length veneer plywood
10. 1/2" x 14" x 12" veneer plywood
11. 1/2" x 3/4" x 1" hardwood
12. 3/4" x 3-1/2" x 13-1/2" hardwood
13. 3/4" x 3" x 4-3/4" hardwood

Palacian: The heavily dramatic aura of the Palacian is an ideal accent that appeals to rich tastes and low budgets.

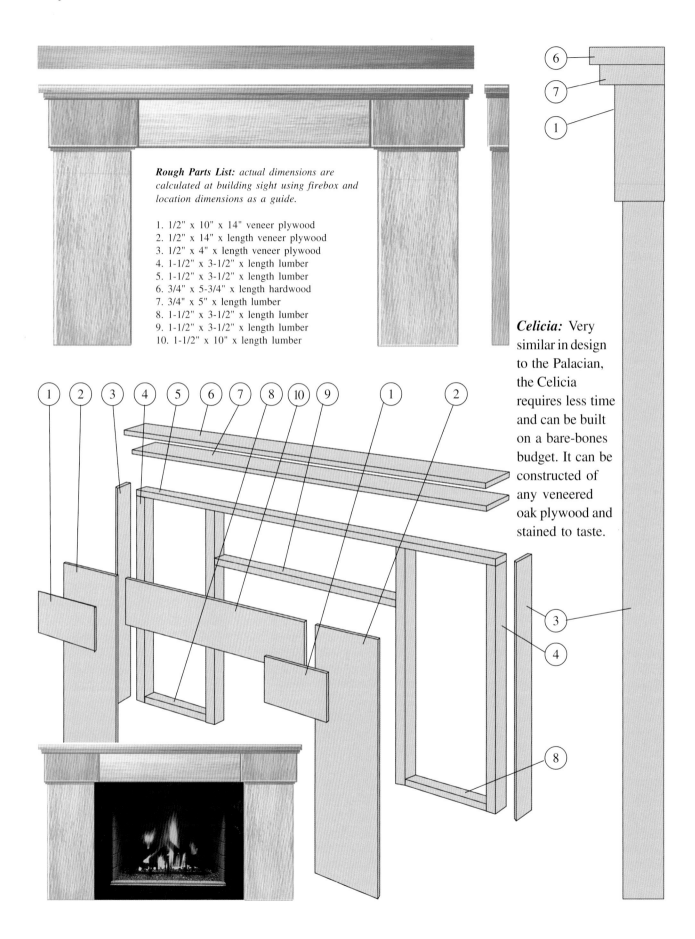

Rough Parts List: *actual dimensions are calculated at building sight using firebox and location dimensions as a guide.*

1. 1/2" x 10" x 14" veneer plywood
2. 1/2" x 14" x length veneer plywood
3. 1/2" x 4" x length veneer plywood
4. 1-1/2" x 3-1/2" x length lumber
5. 1-1/2" x 3-1/2" x length lumber
6. 3/4" x 5-3/4" x length hardwood
7. 3/4" x 5" x length lumber
8. 1-1/2" x 3-1/2" x length lumber
9. 1-1/2" x 3-1/2" x length lumber
10. 1-1/2" x 10" x length lumber

Celicia: Very similar in design to the Palacian, the Celicia requires less time and can be built on a bare-bones budget. It can be constructed of any veneered oak plywood and stained to taste.

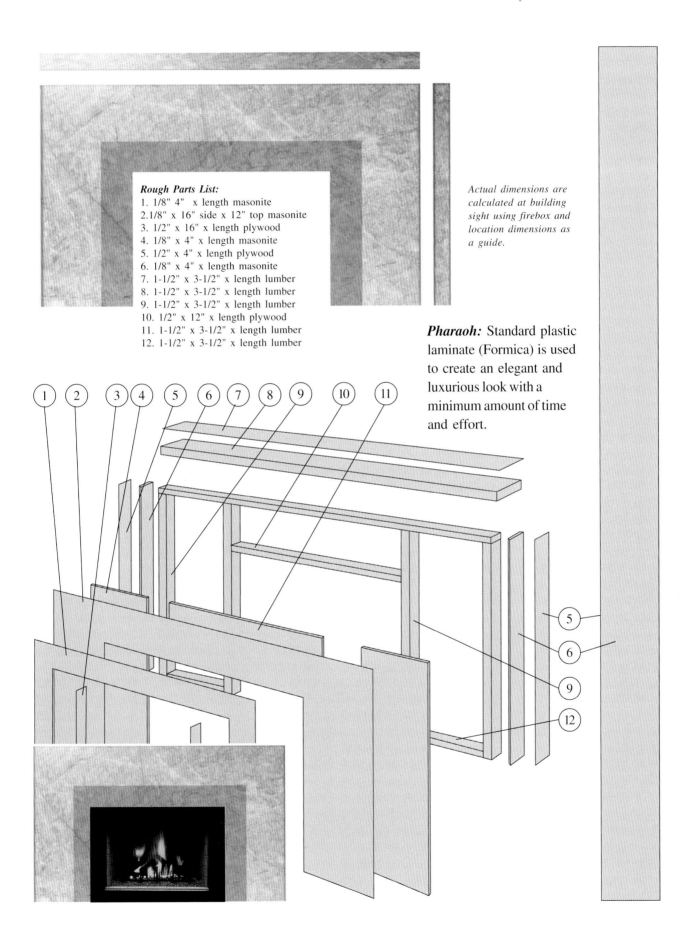

Rough Parts List:
1. 1/8" 4" x length masonite
2. 1/8" x 16" side x 12" top masonite
3. 1/2" x 16" x length plywood
4. 1/8" x 4" x length masonite
5. 1/2" x 4" x length plywood
6. 1/8" x 4" x length masonite
7. 1-1/2" x 3-1/2" x length lumber
8. 1-1/2" x 3-1/2" x length lumber
9. 1-1/2" x 3-1/2" x length lumber
10. 1/2" x 12" x length plywood
11. 1-1/2" x 3-1/2" x length lumber
12. 1-1/2" x 3-1/2" x length lumber

Actual dimensions are calculated at building sight using firebox and location dimensions as a guide.

Pharaoh: Standard plastic laminate (Formica) is used to create an elegant and luxurious look with a minimum amount of time and effort.

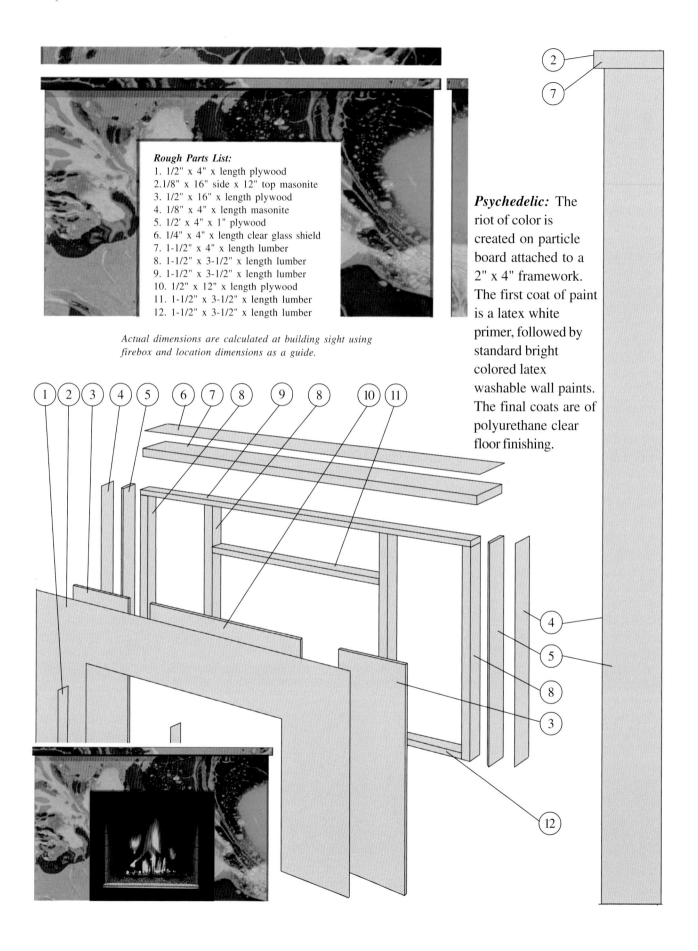

Rough Parts List:
1. 1/2" x 4" x length plywood
2. 1/8" x 16" side x 12" top masonite
3. 1/2" x 16" x length plywood
4. 1/8" x 4" x length masonite
5. 1/2' x 4" x 1" plywood
6. 1/4" x 4" x length clear glass shield
7. 1-1/2" x 4" x length lumber
8. 1-1/2" x 3-1/2" x length lumber
9. 1-1/2" x 3-1/2" x length lumber
10. 1/2" x 12" x length plywood
11. 1-1/2" x 3-1/2" x length lumber
12. 1-1/2" x 3-1/2" x length lumber

Actual dimensions are calculated at building sight using firebox and location dimensions as a guide.

Psychedelic: The riot of color is created on particle board attached to a 2" x 4" framework. The first coat of paint is a latex white primer, followed by standard bright colored latex washable wall paints. The final coats are of polyurethane clear floor finishing.

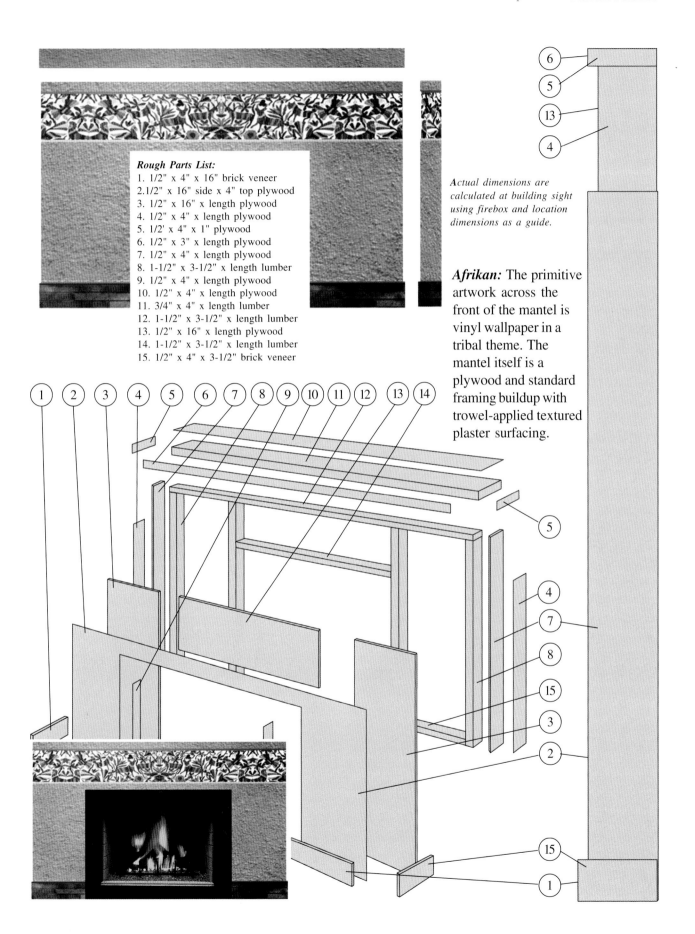

Rough Parts List:
1. 1/2" x 4" x 16" brick veneer
2. 1/2" x 16" side x 4" top plywood
3. 1/2" x 16" x length plywood
4. 1/2" x 4" x length plywood
5. 1/2' x 4" x 1" plywood
6. 1/2" x 3" x length plywood
7. 1/2" x 4" x length plywood
8. 1-1/2" x 3-1/2" x length lumber
9. 1/2" x 4" x length plywood
10. 1/2" x 4" x length plywood
11. 3/4" x 4" x length lumber
12. 1-1/2" x 3-1/2" x length lumber
13. 1/2" x 16" x length plywood
14. 1-1/2" x 3-1/2" x length lumber
15. 1/2" x 4" x 3-1/2" brick veneer

Actual dimensions are calculated at building sight using firebox and location dimensions as a guide.

Afrikan: The primitive artwork across the front of the mantel is vinyl wallpaper in a tribal theme. The mantel itself is a plywood and standard framing buildup with trowel-applied textured plaster surfacing.

The Savannah Mantel can be varnished, stained or painted to match the decor of any living area..

Chapter Ten

Build a Mantel

Follow these easy steps to create a beautiful quality mantel.

This Savannah style mantel is easy to build and affordable using readily available home supply materials and tools. Basic crafting skills are all that are required to complete this outstanding beauty.

I was pleasantly surprised that I could build this mantel and am thrilled with the results! Most girls are afraid to tackle this big of a project, but the guys in my neighborhood kept daring me to do it. I was pleased that I could build the Savannah Mantel from start-to-finish, by myself, over the weekend.

Using the local builder's supply to purchase clear pine boards, classic molding strips and pre-made appliques, the project was both affordable and fun. I discovered my basic wood working skills were all that was required to achieve professional results.

Materials List:
Molding (see insert)
A. Crown Molding   10'
B. Bull Molding   8'
C. Casement   20'
D. 1/2" quarter rnd. 16'
E. 1" x 12" x 8 ft.   8 pieces
F. 1" x 6" x 6 ft.   8 pieces
G. 2" x 4" x 8 ft.   1 piece
H. 2" x 10" x 10'   1 piece
I. 1" x 8" x 8'   1 piece
2" Finish nails   1 box
1-1/4" Finish nails   1 box
Woodworker's glue   1 bottle
Minwax Polyshade   1 quart
Minwax Putty   1 jar
Wood Screw #8 x 2"   8 pieces

Common Molding Types

B. Bull Molding 8'

A. Crown Molding   10'

C. Casement   20'

The Savannah Mantel is constructed of common home builder's supply materials. The moldings and carvings are all off-the-shelf.

The tools required for constructing the Savannah are from my home tool kit. I made all the cuts with the skill saw, including the required miters on the molding.

Tool List:

Skill Saw
Face Shield
Belt Sander
Nail Punch
Hammer
Putty Knife
Square
3" Paint Brush
Dust Mask

I always use a face shield and dust mask when working with wood.

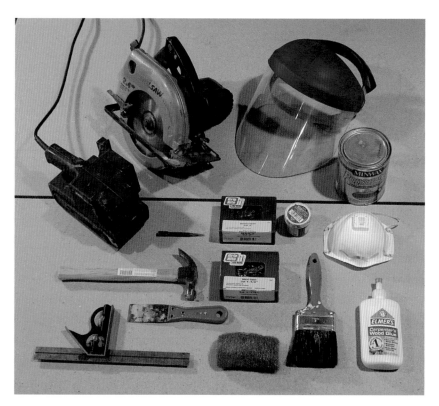

The first step is to build the left and right column boxes. This will provide an easy platform for the remaining construction.

1. Measure 57-1/2" distance for the 4 column sides using 4 pieces of 1" x 6" x 8 ft. lumber.

2. I always use the carpenter's square for a true square cut. Mark all 4 pieces. Each piece is marked at the 57-1/2" distance.

3. Hold the board firmly when using a skill saw. Saw all 4 sides of the columns to length.

4. Edge align 2 column sides on the 1" x 12" lumber and measure the distance inside the column sides.

5. My 1" x 12" boards were only 11-1/4" wide. Saw out 4 pieces of 1" x 6" stock at a length to equal your 1" x 12" width.

6. One 1" x 6" section will be nailed at 4" from the far end and one is nailed at 45" from the far end of 2 of the column sides.

7. Glue and nail the two support pieces to the column sides. Make sure that the parts are at 90 degree angles in both directions.

8. Run a bead of glue along the top edges of the assembly. Include the 2 short legs that are nailed to the long member.

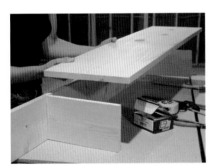

9. Saw a 1" x 12" board 45" long and nail to the face. Align the top of the board with the edge of the short section shown above.

10. Nail in place as shown above. The long side is flush with the edge of the face board. Note the overhang on other side.

11. Run a bead of glue along the board for the second side of the column along with the 2 short legs as shown in photo.

12. Nail the side board to the assembly as shown above. The column now has 2 identical sides and a wide smooth face.

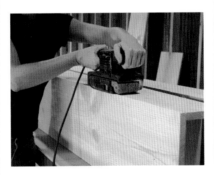

13. The belt sander is ideal for smoothing out the butt joints of the columns. With a little care the seam just disappears.

14. Nail support blocks to inside edge of each column. The blocks are placed 3/4" from the upper cross members.

15. Saw a 1" x 12" board to a length of 82-5/8". This part will the upper face of the fireplace mantel.

16. Align upper face board to the outside edges of the columns. The upper face fits tightly against the column faces.

17. Glue and nail the upper face board to the 2 columns. The columns must be at a 90 degree angle to the upper face board.

18. Measure the inside width of columns. This dimension will be applied to a 1" x 6" board to make the upper face return part.

19. Transfer the dimension to a 1" x 6" board. Use the carpenter's square for a true 90 degree saw cut. Saw to length.

20. Apply glue to the attaching edge of the part and to the receiving edges on the completed mantel assembly.

21. Carefully slide the part into place. Do not get glue on outside surfaces of the mantel or it will repel the final finish.

22. Nail the part into the inside of the assembly. Also drive nails through the front of the mantel into the part.

The basic mantel box is complete. Make sure the columns are at a 90 degree angle with the face. The next step is to measure for building the mantel top cap.

23. Check all the dimensions of the mantel assembly for accuracy. The next step is to make the top cap assembly.

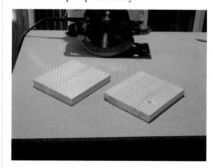

24. The top cap is made of 1" x 8" board. Cheeks are 1" x 6" board and the length of the 1" x 8" board. Make two.

25. Measure width of the mantel assembly to calculate the overall length of the top cap. Add 1-1/2" for cheeks.

26. Glue and nail the top cap face to the two face cheeks as shown above. The assembly is ready for the center section.

27. Measure the inside of the top cap. Saw a 1" x 8" board to this length. The board will be used to make the center section.

29. Place the center section board onto the support blocks. Press it tightly against the face back of the top cap. Nail in place.

31. Saw a 2" x 12" board to a length of 93". Place it flush to the back with an even amount of overhang on each end.

28. Place two stacks of two 3/4" thick blocks about 2 ft. from each cheek. These will support the center section assembly.

30. Place the partially assembled top cap in place on the mantel assembly. It will overhang a little on the front side.

32. Using glue and 3" finish nails, nail the mantel top to the top cap. Make sure that the backside is flush with the top cap.

The assembly is ready for final edge and surface sanding. The belt sander is used to smooth out the butt joints. With a little care the joints will completely vanish and will be as clean as mitered corners.

33. The crown molding is mitered to fit the sides and front of the top cap. I used my skill saw with a finish blade. It works great.

35. The column bases receive cheeks and faces of butt jointed 1" x 12" stock. The cheeks are measured then nailed in place.

37. The column buildups are sawn from the 1" x 6" stock and are 27" in length. These will be enhanced with 1/2" quarter round.

34. The mitered molding is carefully nailed to the top cap with small finish nails. The mantel is really taking shape now.

36. The molding dimensions are directly measured from the columns for a precise miter and exact fit and finish.

38. The column buildup is glued and nailed into place on both columns. The buildup is 16-3/4" from the bottom of the column.

39. The mantel mount blocks are screwed to the wall and the floor. These are positioned to align with the inside cavities and outside edges of the mantel sides. A little trial and error will be required.

40. The mantel is screwed to the mounting blocks through the top sides and base. The bottom molding is then nailed in place.

41. The carved appliques are attached. Sand to prep for varnishing. Use colored Minwax wood filler where required.

42. Three coats of Minwax Polyshade are applied with sanding between coats. Steel wool final coat when dry.

The Savannah Mantel is designed for a 36" wide firebox. The combustible parts must be 12" from the firebox edge.

Superior Fireplace Company

Chapter Eleven

Idea Gallery

Photos of Existing Fireplace Installations

Mantels are an integral part of a home's ambiance. We've put together this assortment of existing photos that cover a wide range of tastes and styles. We hope you enjoy reviewing them as much as we enjoyed compiling the collection.

Doing the research for your own fireplace mantel and then managing the installation yourself is a real pleasure, and whether you build or buy, the results are happily rewarding. There is nothing quite as satisfying as personally creating an addition to your home or special living space that you and your loved ones can enjoy for years to come.

What's more, adding a new fireplace to your home is a surefire way to increase its value.

When planning your installation, take advantage of resources available at local fireplace dealers. Their help is priceless.

Visit hazelmeremantels.com for more of the latest mantel designs like these shown above.

Visit wohners.com for more of the latest mantel designs like these shown above.

Fireplace Dealers and Suppliers

United States and Canada

Local dealers are your best bet for obtaining quality assistance when planning for a fireplace mantel or a complete installation. Using their expertise helps create a project that is safe, economical and an improvement to the quality and value of your home *(suppliers on page 130)*.

ALABAMA

TUSCALOOSA INTERIORS
3100 25TH AVE, SUITE C
TUSCALOOSA, AL 35401
Phone: 205-750-3151

ALASKA

FIREPLACE GALLERY
852 W INTERNATIONAL
AIRPORT RD
SUITE 101
ANCHORAGE, AK 99518
Phone: 907-240-5337

HARDY HEATING, INC
3101 N DOLLY VARDEN DR
WASILLA, AK 99687
Phone: 907-373-2580

ALBERTA

MR. FIREPLACE
5410 17TH AVENUE
CALGARY, AB T2A 0W1
Phone: 403-272-5055

VAGLIO FIREPLACES
5718 GATEWAY BLVD
EDMONTON, AB T6H 5E4
Phone: 780-435-3521

ARIZONA

BANKER INSULATION
1590 COPPER RD
LAKE HAVASU, AZ 86404
Phone: 928-680-4888

BANKER INSULATION
5790 FULTON RD
PRESCOTT VALLEY,
AZ 86314
Phone: 928-772-2544

BANKER INSULATION
2601 VERBENA AVE
TUCSON, AZ 85705
Phone: 520-293-5815

ARKANSAS

ALLIED EQUIPMENT & SUPPLY
26096 INTERSTATE 30
ALEXANDER, AR 72002
Phone: 501-847-3582

KOZY HEAT FIREPLACES
13080 N HWY 71
BENTONVILLE, AR 72712
Phone: 479-464-0098

BRITISH COLUMBIA

POINTWEST SERVICES LTD
805 NOTRE DAME DR #101
KAMLOOPS, BC V2C 5N8
Phone: 250-374-0919

A R DYCK HEATING LTD
1980 SPRINGFIELD RD
KELOWNA, BC V1Y 5V7
Phone: 250-860-6556

HECTORS HEATING & VENTILATION
2031 MALAVIEW AVE
W #203
SIDNEY, BC V8L 5X6
Phone: 250-655-0661

CALIFORNIA

FIREPLACE DEPOT
1220 SAN JUAN RD
HOLLISTER, CA 95023
Phone: 831-636-5400

ALL YEAR HEATING
& AIR CONDITIONING
801 PLAZA AVE
SACRAMENTO, CA 95815
Phone: 916-922-7796

WALKER-MC DONALD
3618 BROADWAY
SACRAMENTO, CA 95817
Phone: 916-456-4738

TOP QUALITY INSULATION
& FIREPLACE
105 MAIN ST
VALLEY SPRINGS,
CA 95252
Phone: 209-772-2501

ARMAND'S
9400 VENICE BLVD.
CULVER CITY, CA 90232
Phone: 310-839-5555

GIDDEN BROTHERS
232 S LINCOLN WAY
GALT, CA 95632
Phone: 209-745-1700

BENS APPLIANCE
1535 S. CHEROKEE
LODI, CA 95240
Phone: 209-369-4716

SKELTON HEATING
5431 GRANTLINE RD
TRACY, CA 95376
Phone: 209-832-7602

COLORADO

SNOOZEASE HOME
HEARTH OUTFITTERS
999 E EVANS AVE
DENVER, CO 80210
Phone: 303-722-6698

BOULDER STOVE
AND FLOORING
2868 30TH ST
BOULDER, CO 80301
Phone: 303-442-4324

THE FIREPLACE CO
1705 AIRPORT RD
BRECKENRIDGE,
CO 80424
Phone: 970-453-2212

AIR O THERM
1315 W EDISON ST
BRUSH, CO 80723-2309
Phone: 970-842-0400

ROCKY MOUNTAIN
HOME SERVICES INC
244 MAIN ST
CANON CITY, CO 81212
Phone: 719-275-6534

FIREPLACE WEST II
1408 RIVERSIDE AVE
FORT COLLINS, CO 80524
Phone: 970-498-9679

HARBERT LUMBER CO
240 NORTH AVE
GRAND JUNCTION,
CO 81502-0458
Phone: 970-243-3273

D J HANNON GAS SHOP
1930 E BOULDER
COLORADO SPRINGS,
CO 80909
Phone: 719-577-9488

PARKER HEATING
& AIR CONDITIONING
206 E NORTH
P O BOX 271
LAMAR, CO 81052
Phone: 719-336-4758

THE HEARTH EXCHANGE
23698 N HWY 24 STE D-2
MINTURN, CO 81645
Phone: 970-827-9623

SPA BROKERS II
8791 WEDSWORTH BVD
WESTMINSTER,
CO 80003
Phone: 303-420-1040

CONNECTICUT

FIREPLACES & STOVES
1457 MERIDEN
WATERBURY RD
MILLDALE, CT 06467
Phone: 860-620-5555

PAPAS HEARTH & HOME
249-251 WEST MAIN ST
BUILDING 1, UNIT 5
BRANFORD, CT 06405
Phone: 203-483-9461

NOVICKY INC.
75 GRAYS BRIDGE RD
BROOKFIELD, CT 06804
Phone: 203-775-2367

THE WARMING ZONE
234 MIDDLE ST
MIDDLETOWN, CT 06457
Phone: 860-347-8844

ADVANCED GAS
SALES & SERVICE
183 E HADDAM RD
SALEM, CT 06420
Phone: 860-859-9070

DELAWARE

COMFORT ONE
990 BALTIMORE PIKE
GLEN MILLS, PA 19342
Phone: 610-459-4665

FLORIDA

A PLUS FIREPLACES
8133 RIDGE RD.
PORT RICHEY, FL 34668
Phone: 727-847-6248

MR. FIREPLACE
3351 W. NEWHAVEN AVE
STE 101
MELBOURNE, FL 32904
Phone: 321-727-7565

ACCENT FIREPLACES
& ACCESSORIES L.L.C.
4150 HANCOCK
BRIDGE PKWY
UNIT 6 & 7
NORTH FT MYERS,
FL 33903
Phone: 239-656-3473

FOUR SEASONS
GAS SERVICE
3975 FORRESTAL AVE #100
ORLANDO, FL 32806
Phone: 407-859-5424

COASTAL INSULATION
8006 PITTMAN AVE.
PENSACOLA, FL 32534
Phone: 850-476-7778

ALLGAS CO
6805 HWY 301 S
RIVERVIEW,
FL 33569-4340
Phone: 813-741-2595

INTERIOR BUILDING
SPECIALTIES
595 6TH ST NW
WINTER HAVEN, FL 33881
Phone: 863-293-4295

GEORGIA

RESIDENTIAL CONST
6582 PEACHTREE
INDUSTRIAL BLVD
PO BOX 2067
NORCROSS, GA 30091
Phone: 770-368-0646

HEARTH & PATIO
2316 MAIN ST
TUCKER, GA 30084
Phone: 770-934-8646

CHEROKEE HEARTH AND HOME
1257 AUGUSTA
W PARKWAY
AUGUSTA, GA 30906
Phone: 706-854-1181

RCS HIRAM
1665 HIRAM
DOUGLASVILLE HWY
HIRAM, GA 30141
Phone: 770-943-7350

AMERICAN SPCLTS CO
4408 COLUMBUS RD
MACON, GA 31212
Phone: 478-474-0074

HOME SPECIALTY
& DESIGN CENTER
107 SOUTH CORDER RD
WARNER ROBBINS,
GA 31088
Phone: 478-975-0720

FINES GAS APPLIANCE
2364 LAFAYETTE RD
OGELTHORPE, GA 30742
Phone: 706-866-8290

IDAHO

FIREPLACE SHOP
2130 SOUTH YELLOWSTONE
IDAHO FALLS, ID 83402
Phone: 208-523-1199

A-1 FIREPLACE
5880 W FRANKLIN RD
BOISE, ID 83709
Phone: 208-345-1992

LARRYS ELECTRIC
& HEATING
1133 ALBION AVE
BURLEY, ID 83318
Phone: 208-678-4071

ILLINOIS

SOUTHWEST
FIREPLACE
431 S ROUTE 59
AURORA, IL 60504
Phone: 630-851-9800

HOUSE OF
FIREPLACES
1255 BOWES ROAD
ELGIN, IL 60123
Phone: 847-741-6464

BARNETTS HOUSE
OF FIREPLACES INC
1620 5TH AVE
MOLINE, IL 61265
Phone: 309-762-8030

SOUTHWEST
FIREPLACES
11921 SOUTH 80TH AVE
PALOS PARK, IL 60464
Phone: 708-448-3883

MAZE LUMBER
1100 WATER ST
PERU, IL 61354
Phone: 815-223-1742

PETER'S HEATING
& AIR COND.
4520 BROADWAY
QUINCY, IL 62301
Phone: 217-222-1368

ANSELMO'S
1235 W LE FEVRE RD
STERLING, IL 61081
Phone: 815-625-3519

FIREPLACE
SPECIALISTS INC
610 PLAZA DR UNIT 5
SYCAMORE, IL 60178
Phone: 815-899-6615

GRASS ROOTS
ENERGY
28751 N RAND ROAD
WAUCONDA, IL 60084
Phone: 847-526-5888

PETERS HEATING
& AIR CONDITIONING
1401 W WASHINGTON
PITTSFIELD, IL 62363
Phone: 217-285-1600

BENSON STONE CO.
1100 11TH ST
ROCKFORD, IL 61104
Phone: 815-227-2000

BOETTNER CO INC
206 E STEPHENSON ST
FREEPORT, IL 61032
Phone: 815-235-6000

INDIANA

STONEWALL MSNRY
INC FIREMASTERS
1235 W HIVELY
ELKHART, IN 46517
Phone: 574-522-5200

NOB BRICK
4936 NOB ROAD
FORT WAYNE, IN 46825
Phone: 219-483-2126

HENRY POOR
LUMBER
3200 REAGAN DR
LAFAYETTE, IN 47909
Phone: 765-474-1388

HOOSIER HEARTH
613 N MADISON ST
MUNCIE, IN 47305
Phone: 765-289-0681

STONEWALL
FIREPLACE & STONE
1152 MARSH ST STE A
VALPARAISO, IN 46385
Phone: 219-548-3555

FIREPLACE
& GAS CENTER
6442 PENDLETON AVE
ANDERSON, IN 46013
Phone: 765-642-9946

FIREPLACE CENTER
1210 W 2ND ST
BLOOMINGTON,
IN 47403
Phone: 812-336-2053

BASSEMIERS
FIREPLACE & PATIO
4220 E MORGAN AVE
EVANSVILLE, IN 47715
Phone: 812-479-6338

KINGS HEATING
& PLUMBING
115 E VAILE AVE
KOKOMO, IN 46901
Phone: 765-457-6664

SCULLYS
FIREPLACE SHOP
1385 S 10TH ST
NOBLESVILLE,
IN 46060
Phone: 317-776-9445

HEARTH
& HOME SHOPPE
11130 W 93RD AVE
ST JOHN, IN 46373
Phone: 219-365-9975

FIREPLACE WORLD
2016 WABASH AVE
TERRE HAUTE, IN 47807
Phone: 812-235-5815

OLD SMOKEYS
ENERGY
ALTERNATIVE
3346 COUNTY RD OO
ASHLEY, IN 46705
Phone: 260-587-9691

LAFAYETTE
MASONRY SUPPLY
1799 N 9TH ST
LAFAYETTE, IN 47904
Phone: 765-742-0146

HITZER INC
269 E MAIN
BERNE, IN 46711
Phone: 260-589-8536

FIREPLACE
BUILDERS
OF INDIANA
2662 N MORTON
FRANKLIN, IN 46131
Phone: 317-346-6005

FLOWER STALL
HEARTH & HOME
347 US 231 SO
SOUTHGATE CENTER
JASPER, IN 47546
Phone: 812-482-1213

WIEDEMAN HEATING
& ELECTRIC
125 N MERIDIAN
SUNMAN, IN 47041
Phone: 812-623-2201

HERITAGE
COMPANIES
750 OLD WHTLND RD
VINCENNIS, IN 47591
Phone: 812-886-4083

IOWA

RALSTON CREEK
2301 HWY 6 WEST
CORALVILLE, IA 52241
Phone: 319-351-2189

BIRCH FIREPLACE & PATIO
365 CEDAR CROSS RD
DUBUQUE, IA 52003
Phone: 563-588-9978

RALSTON CREEK
1095 NORTH
CENTER POINT RD
HIAWATHA, IA 52233
Phone: 319-393-3838

FIREPLACE
SUPER STORE
10870 DOUGLAS AVE
URBANDALE, IA 50322
Phone: 515-270-5377

FIREPLACE PROS
1217 W 41ST ST
SIOUX FALLS, SD 57105
Phone: 605-339-0775

NORTH IOWA
LUMBER
1621 HIGHWAY 18
ALGONA, IA 50511
Phone: 515-295-7239

LITZEL LUMBER
3705 W LINCOLN WAY
AMES, IA 50014-3495
Phone: 515-292-1262

ABBAS FLOORING
& FIREPLACES
223 EAST MAIN ST
BELMOND, IA 50421
Phone: 641-444-7218

DENNYS HEATING
& AIR COND
217 W MAPLE
CHEROKEE, IA 51012
Phone: 712-225-4650

NORDIC HEARTH
1785 STATE HWY 9
DECORAH, IA 52101
Phone: 563-382-4168

COLONIAL
FIREPLACE
216 N 12TH ST
FORT DODGE, IA 50501
Phone: 515-576-8116

HOME LUMBER
716 S JEFFERSON
MASON CITY, IA 50401
Phone: 641-424-4001

UNITED BUILDING CTR
2210 EAST 4TH ST
SIOUX CITY, IA 51106
Phone: 712-255-3508

UNITED BUILDING CTR
1008 18TH ST
SPRIT LAKE, IA 51360
Phone: 712-336-1514

TRI-STATE STOVE WRK
1094 240TH AVE
WESTPOINT, IA 52656
Phone: 319-837-6992

BARNETTS HOUSE OF FIREPLACES
1620 5TH AVE
MOLINE, IL 61265
Phone: 309-762-8030

FIRESIDE HEARTH & HOME ROSEVILLE
2700 N FAIRVIEW AVE
ROSEVILLE, MN 55113
Phone: 651-633-1042

CHASE LUMBER
1315 ALBANY PLACE SE
ORANGE CITY,
IA 51041-0138
Phone: 712-737-8857

TRI STATE WINDOW
& POOL
1106 MAIN
KEOKUK, IA 52632
Phone: 319-524-4551

KANSAS

STAR LUMBER
902 INDIANAPOLIS
WICHITA, KS 67211
Phone: 316-941-1860

WESTERN
FIREPLACE SUPPLY
4244 NE PORT DR
LEES SUMMIT, MO 64064
Phone: 800-530-8929

UBC UNITED
BLDING CENTER
1514 E FULTON
GARDEN CITY, KS 67846
Phone: 620-275-7411

EBELING POOLS
513 SOUTH WALNUT
HUTCHINSON, KS 67501
Phone: 316-663-9805

ENERGY CENTER
528 PILLSBURY DR
MANHATTAN, KS 66502
Phone: 785-776-5118

KANSAS CITY
BUILDING SUPPLY
7600 WEDD RD
OVERLAND PARK,
KS 66204
Phone: 913-962-5227

KENTUCKY

DAYTON
FIREPLACE SYSTEMS.
450 GARGRAVE RD
WEST CARROLLTON,
OH 45449
Phone: 937-847-8139

BASSEMIERS
FIREPLACE & PATIO
4220 E MORGAN AVE
EVANSVILLE, IN 47715
Phone: 812-479-6338

FIREPLACE
OF NORTHERN KY
10135 DIXIE HWY
FLORENCE, KY 41042
Phone: 859-746-3473

FIREPLACE DIST
OF BLUEGRASS
125A TRADE ST
LEXINGTON, KY 40510
Phone: 859-233-1039

FIREPLACE
DISTRIBUTORS
5810 FERN VALLEY RD
LOUISVILLE, KY 40228
Phone: 502-964-5996

MAINE

FINEST KIND
9 COMMERCIAL ST
PORTLAND, ME 04101
Phone: 207-772-2155

BLACK STOVE SHOP
893 US RT 1
YARMOUTH, ME 04096
Phone: 207-846-9030

SUNRISE HOME
& HEARTH
753 STILLWATER AVE
BANGOR, ME 04401
Phone: 207-942-4231

WADES STOVE BARN
RR3 BOX 3897 RTE 137
WINSLOW, ME 04901
Phone: 207-859-9773

MANITOBA

FLAME & COMFORT
318 LOGAN AVE
SILVANIA ITALIA LTD
WINNIPEG, MB R3A 0P5
Phone: 204-943-5263

MARYLAND

ACE HARDWARE
& HEARTH
7936 CRAIN HWY SO
PARK 97 CENTER
GLEN BURNIE,
MD 21061
Phone: 410-969-5050

ACME STOVES
15221 DISPLAY COURT
ROCKVILLE, MD 20850
Phone: 301-309-1998

WARNERS STOVE SHOP
1201 VIRGINIA AVE
CUMBERLAND,
MD 21502
Phone: 301-724-0774

FIREPLACE SHOP
EASY FIRE SUPPLY
16165 SHADY GROVE
GAITHERSBURG,
MD 20877
Phone: 301-990-6195

ACE HARDWARE
4167 MOUNTAIN ROAD
PASADENA, MD 21122
Phone: 410-437-4300

BELAIR ENGINEERING
15881 COMMERCE CT
UPPER MARLBORO,
MD 20774
Phone: 301-249-0300

TOLBARD GAS
FIREPLACE SHOP
1782 NORTH MARKET ST
FREDERICK, MD 21701
Phone: 301-662-2515

WATSONS
FIREPLACE & PATIO
1616 YORK RD
LUTHERVILLE,
MD 21093
Phone: 410-321-5855

FIRESIDE
HEARTH & HOME
22 IRONGATE DRIVE
WALDORF, MD 20602
Phone: 301-638-5858

FIREPLACE SUPPLY CO
5807 GEORGE
ISLAND LANDING RD
STOCKTON, MD 21864
Phone: 410-632-9944

MASSACHUSETTS

YANKEE FIREPLACE
& GRILL CITY
140 S MAIN ST.
MIDDLETON, MA 01949
Phone: 978-774-2760

ROSE FORGE
320 UNDERPASS RD
BREWSTER, MA 02631
Phone: 508-896-6505

BLACK MAGIC
FIREPLACE SHOP
21 NEW ST
CAMBRIDGE, MA 02138
Phone: 617-876-4456

CHELMSFORD
FIREPLACE
73 SUMMER ST
CHEMSFORD, MA 01824
Phone: 978-256-6328

WOODSTOVES &
FIREPLACES UNLTD.
193 E. GROVE ST.
MIDDLEBORO, MA 02346
Phone: 508-947-8835

STOVE PLACE
95 HARTFORD TURNPIKE
SHREWSBURY, MA 01545
Phone: 508-754-7091

BOSTON FIREPLACE
HYDRO THERAPY
1107 COMMONWEALTH AVE
BOSTON, MA 02215
Phone: 617-787-5000

EN-R-GY SAVERS
1470 WASHINGTON ST.
HOLLISTON, MA 01746
Phone: 508-429-2008

IRON HOUSE INC
95 CORPORATION ROAD
HYANNIS, MA 02601
Phone: 508-771-4799

FIRESIDE DESIGNS
1458 RIVERDALE ST
WEST SPRINGFIELD,
MA 01089
Phone: 413-733-0910

STOVE DEPOT
HEARTH & HOME
1049 TURNPIKE ST
CANTON, MA 02021
Phone: 781-821-0777

FEENS COUNTRY
LIVING INC
975 MERRIAM AVE
TWIN CITY MALL
LEOMINSTER, MA 01453
Phone: 978-537-4518

GRILL WORLD PLUS
326 MAIN ST
NORTHBOROUGH,
MA 01532
Phone: 508-393-2424

SIPPICAN STOVE
129 MARION RD
WAREHAM, MA 02571
Phone: 508-291-0300

MICHIGAN

FIRESIDE
HEARTH & HOME
42647 FORD RD
CANTON, MI 48187
Phone: 734-981-4700

HEARTHCREST
2176 WEALTHY ST SE
GRAND RAPIDS, MI 49506
Phone: 616-456-5300

MODERN HARDWARE
1500 KALMAZO AVE SE
GRAND RAPIDS, MI 49507
Phone: 616-241-2655

A-1 MECHANICAL
4428 S CREYTS
LANSING, MI 48917
Phone: 517-322-2300

PINE TREE
HEATING & A/C
404 W NEPESSING
LAPEER, MI 48466
Phone: 810-667-3778

REC ROOM
2322 US HWY 41 W
MARQUETTE, MI 49855
Phone: 906-266-6630

HEARTH-N-HOME
6990 W M-21
OWOSSO, MI 48867
Phone: 989-723-2177

HEARTH-N-HOME
102 N MAIN
PERRY, MI 48872
Phone: 517-625-5586

FIRESIDE
HEARTH & HOME
23600 TELEGRAPH RD
SOUTHFIELD, MI 48034
Phone: 248-354-3511

PHILLIPS ENERGY INC
989 S AIRPORT RD W
TRAVERSE CITY,
MI 49686
Phone: 231-929-1396

HOLLY'S SHOWCASE
& MOWER INC
6898 WEST MONROE RD
ONSTED, MI 49265
Phone: 517-467-9029

LAKESHORE
CEMENT PRODUCTS
5251 N US 23
OSCODA, MI 48750
Phone: 989-739-9341

BLUEWATER HEARTH & HOME
1439 PINE GROVE AVE
PORT HURON, MI 48060
Phone: 810-987-3627

EMMETT'S ENERGY
70790 VANDYKE
ROMEO, MI 48065
Phone: 586-752-2075

ELLIOTT HEATING
562 E SPRUCE ST
SAULT SAINTE MARIE, MI 49783
Phone: 906-632-9700

PHILLIPS ENERGY
GRAND TRAVERSE ML
3200 S. AIRPORT RD
SUITE 130
TRAVERSE CITY, MI 49686
Phone: 231-935-4428

EMMETT'S ENERGY
4994 DIXIE HIGHWAY
WATERFORD, MI 48329
Phone: 248-674-3828

SHOWCASE CABINETS
3142 N ADRIAN HWY
ADRIAN, MI 49221
Phone: 517-264-6531

SOLLEYS INC
3779 M-15
CLARKSTON, MI 48348
Phone: 248-625-2417

ROYAL FIREPLACE
INDUSTRIAL DR
JENISON, MI 49428
Phone: 616-669-9090

THE FIREPLACE SHOP
13233 W MICHIGAN AVE
MARSHALL, MI 49068
Phone: 269-781-4064

BEACH HOME
& HEARTH
9776 EAST D
AVENUE AT M-89
RICHLAND, MI 49083
Phone: 269-629-5531

MR. FIREPLACE
5060 JACKSON RD
ANN ARBOR, MI 48103
Phone: 734-213-2737

LINDSAY HEATING
3735 COMMERCE
JACKSON, MI 49203
Phone: 517-748-9155

MINNESOTA

FIRESIDE HEARTH & HOME
3850 W HWY 13
BURNSVILLE, MN 55337
Phone: 612-890-0758

CONDOR FIREPLACE
8282 ARTHUR ST NE
SPRING LAKE PARK,
MN 55432
Phone: 763-786-2341

FIRESIDE
HEARTH & HOME
109 4TH ST NE
ST CLOUD, MN 56387
Phone: 320-251-2717

FIREPLACE
PROFESSIONALS, INC
1217 W 41ST ST
SIOUX FALLS, SD 57105
Phone: 605-339-0775

JIM & DUDES
PLUMBING & HEATING
724 WEST CLARK ST
ALBERT LEA, MN 56007
Phone: 507-373-6161

DJ'S FIREPLACE
6060 LABEAUX
ALBERTVILLE,
MN 55301
Phone: 763-497-5313

GREENMAN HEATING
& REFRIGERATION
1001 4TH ST SE
AUSTIN, MN 55912
Phone: 507-437-6500

HILL'S PLUMBING
& HEATING
3801 BEMIDJI AVE N
LONE PINE PLAZA
SUITE 1
BEMIDJI, MN 56601
Phone: 218-751-1286

NORTHLAND
BRICK & FIREPLACE
2111 FORTHUN RD S
BRAINERD
BAXTER, MN 56425
Phone: 218-829-1929

CORNERSTONE
FIREPLACES
107 NORTH MAIN ST
CAMBRIDGE, MN 55008
Phone: 763-689-2876

STREITZ HEATING
708 SCHILLING DR
DUNDAS, MN 55019

CORNERSTONE
525 HAT TRICK AVE HWT 53
EVELETH, MN 55734
Phone: 218-744-3091

FIRESIDE
HEARTH & HOME
1420 N RIVERFRONT DR
MANKATO, MN 56001
Phone: 507-345-8084

COUNTRYSIDE
HEATING
6511 HWY 12
MAPLE PLAIN, MN 55359
Phone: 612-479-1600

FIRESIDE
HEARTH & HOME
225 COUNTY RD 81
OSSEO, MN 55369
Phone: 612-425-9656

FIRESIDE
HEARTH & HOME
2700 N FAIRVIEW AVE
ROSEVILLE, MN 55113
Phone: 651-633-1042

FIRESIDE
HEARTH & HOME
1001 EAST HWY 12
WILLMAR, MN 56201
Phone: 320-235-7415

THE FIREPLACE STORE
2510 BROADWAY ST S
ALEXANDRIA, MN 56308
Phone: 320-762-8645

TOTAL COMFORT
300 DOWNTOWN PLAZA
FAIRMONT, MN 56031
Phone: 507-235-5278

CONTROLLED AIR
21210 EATON AVE
FARMINGTON,
MN 55024
Phone: 651-460-6022

TRUE VALUE
HOME CENTER
HWY 59 N BOX 831
MARSHALL, MN 56258
Phone: 507-532-3296

MISSISSIPPI

BMC SALES
HWY 145 SOUTH
SALTILLO, MS 38866
Phone: 662-869-2619

SANDERS GAS
611 22 AVENUE SOUTH
MERIDEN, MS 39301
Phone: 601-693-4054

MISSOURI

COMPLETE
HOME CONCEPTS
123 NE 91ST ST
KANSAS CITY, MO 64155
Phone: 816-468-0888

WESTERN
FIREPLACE SUPPLY
4244 NE PORT DR
LEES SUMMIT, MO 64064
Phone: 800-530-8929

SHOWCASE
BUILDERS SUPPLY
1211 EAGLECREST ST
NIXA, MO 65714
Phone: 417-725-8090

FIRESIDE SHOPPE
300 N. KINGS HIGHWAY
CAPE GIRARDEAU,
MO 63701
Phone: 573-332-1434

STAR HEATING
AND AIR CONDITIONING
1702 COMMERCE CT
COLUMBIA, MO 65202
Phone: 573-449-3784

HARRIS
HEATING & COOLING
415 W KARSCH BLVD
FARMINGTON,
MO 63640-0737
Phone: 573-756-429

EAST PERRY BLDG SUPPLY
250 WEST ST
FROHNA, MO 63748
Phone: 573-824-5248

PETERS HEATING
& AIR CONDITIONING
4560 PARIS-GRAVEL RD
HANNIBAL, MO 63401
Phone: 573-221-0093

SUPERIOR HEATING
& COOLING
3526 MARKET ST
HANNIBAL, MO 63401
Phone: 573-221-0600

BOGG STEEL & STOVE
3518 N TEN MILE DRIVE
JEFFERSON CITY,
MO 65109
Phone: 573-893-2525

BOGG STEEL & STOVE
3518 N. 10 MILE DR
JEFFERSON CITY, MO 65109
Phone: 573-893-2525

PETERS HEATING
& AIR CONDITIONING
1515 S BALTIMORE
KIRKSVILLE, MO 63501
Phone: 660-665-5665

CLEMENS
POLS & SPAS
RT 4 BOX 140 HWY 240
MARSHALL, MO 65340
Phone: 660-886-7613

NEW HAMPTON
HARDWARE
206 E LINCOLN ST
BOX 287
NEW HAMPTON, MO 64471
Phone: 660-439-3245

HACKMANN LUMBER
2601 HWY K
O FALLON, MO 63366
Phone: 314-240-8360

BUSCH FURNITURE
12345 S HWY 63
ROLLA, MO 65401
Phone: 573-364-8022

HACKMANNS
LUMBER
3030 HWY 94
ST. CHARLES, MO 63303
Phone: 636-441-0100

OUTDOOR POWER
EQUIP & FIREPLACE
510 S 4TH ST
ST. GENEVIEVE,
MO 63670
Phone: 573-883-2845

PETERS HEATING
& AIR CONDITIONING
377 TRAVIS BLVD
TROY, MO 63379
Phone: 636-462-5161

HEARTH & HOME
556 E 5TH ST
WASHINGTON, MO 63090
Phone: 636-390-4242

KANSAS CITY
BUILDING SUPPLY
7600 WEDD RD
OVERLAND PARK,
KS 66204
Phone: 913-962-5227

AIRCO
913 N ELSON
KIRKSVILLE, MO 63501
Phone: 660-665-5597

MONTANA
FIREPLACE CENTER
2304 NORTH 7TH
SUITE H2
BOZEMAN, MT 59715
Phone: 406-522-9160

FIREPLACE CENTER
824 CENTRAL AVE
BILLINGS, MT 59102
Phone: 406-259-9690

AIR CONTROLS
7510 SHEDHORN DR
BOZEMAN, MT 59718
Phone: 406-587-6292

GINNATY HEATING
1425 18TH AVE S
GREAT FALLS, MT 59405
Phone: 406-452-7665

THOMAS PLUMBING
& HEATING
2327 SOUTH AVE WEST
MISSOULA, MT 59801
Phone: 406-728-0216

NEBRASKA

LUMBERMEN'S
BRICK & SUPPLY
1612 SOUTH WEBB ROAD
GRAND ISLAND, NE 68803
Phone: 308-398-5252

LUMBERMEN'S
BRICK & SUPPLY
13709 INDUSTRIAL RD
OMAHA, NE 68137
Phone: 402-894-2222

CAPITAL PATIO
THE FLAME SHOP
5500 OLD CHENEY RD
STE 16
LINCOLN, NE 68516
Phone: 402-421-7575

DOUGLAS HEARTH SHOPPE
5601 S 56TH
ALAMO PLAZA
LINCOLN, NE 68516
Phone: 402-421-8500

PLATTE
CONSTRUCTION
220 W FRONT ST
NORTH PLATTE, NE 69103
Phone: 308-534-2150

NEVADA

FIREPLACE
DISTRIBUTOR NV
120 A WOODLAND AVE
RENO, NV 89523-8909
Phone: 775-747-1346

L & S AIR
CONDITIONING
90 SUNPAC AVE
HENDERSON, NV 89015
Phone: 702-566-1437

GARAGE DOOR
CENTER
1195 GREG ST
SPARKS, NV 89431
Phone: 775-356-3667

NEW BRUNSWICK

HEARTH TECH
TORONTO
6411 EDWARDS BLVD
MISSISSAUGA,
ON L5T 2P7
Phone: 905-696-9991

NEW HAMPSHIRE

FIREPLACE VILLAGE
RT 101 STATE RTE 196
BEDFORD, NH 03110
Phone: 603-472-5626

FIREPLACE VILLAGE
8 LOUDON RD
CONCORD, NH 03301
Phone: 603-228-5578

STOVE SHOPPE
THE COMMONS
25 INDIAN ROCK
RD SUITE 19
WINDHAM, NH 03087
Phone: 603-537-0555

YANKEE COUNTRY
LIVING CENTER
114 LAFAYETTE RD
HAMPTON FALLS,
NH 03844
Phone: 603-926-2424

VERMONT CASTINGS
FACTORY STORE
PENNICHUCK SQUARE
RTE 101 A AMHERST ST
MERRIMACK, NH 03054
Phone: 603-882-7402

WOODMANS FORGE
& FIREPLACE
579 PINE RIVER PND RD
WAKEFIELD, NH 03830
Phone: 603-522-3028

HOME COMFORT
P O 4289 1401 RT 14
WHITE RIVER JUNCTION,
VT 05001
Phone: 802-295-8778

NORDIC STOVE SHOP
75 DOVER POINT RD.
DOVER, NH 03820
Phone: 603-749-4660

ENERGY SAVERS, INC
163 DANIEL WEBSTER HWY
MEREDITH, NH 03253
Phone: 603-279-7961

WOODSVILL STOVE
10 CONNECTICUT ST
WOODSVILLE, NH 03785
Phone: 603-747-3494

NEW JERSEY

CROWN HEARTH
& PATIO
3494 RT 9 S
FREEHOLD, NJ 07728
Phone: 732-866-8700

BRIGHT ACRE
2001 HWY 34
& ALLAIRE RD
WALL TOWNSHIP,NJ 07719
Phone: 732-974-0110

STAR DISTRIBUTORS
1512 S. BLACK
HORSE PIKE
WILLIAMSTOWN,
NJ 08094
Phone: 856-728-4444

NEW MEXICO

GOLDEN FLAME
DISTRIBUTING
15855 N. GREENWAY
HAYDEN LOOP
SCOTTSDALE, AZ 85260
Phone: 480-948-9919

ALBUQUERQUE
FIREPLACE
10415 COMANCHE NE
ALBUQUERQUE,
NM 87111
Phone: 505-323-9864

WESTERN
BUILDING SUPPLY
4201 PASEO DEL NORTE NE
ALBUQUERQUE, NM 87113
Phone: 505-823-2500

WESTERN STOVES
& SPA
1103 E LOHMAN AVE
LAS CRUCES,
NM 88001-3268
Phone: 505-526-5380

NEW YORK

FIREPLACE DIST
6563 TRANSIT RD SO
LOCKPORT, NY 14094
Phone: 716-625-6141

DELFINO INSULATION
104 O HARE RD
MIDDLETOWN, NY 10941
Phone: 845-692-2039

FIREPLACE FASHIONS
1936 HUDSON AVE.
ROCHESTER, NY 14617
Phone: 585-266-8967

FIRE GLOW
1565 RICHMOND RD
STATEN ISLAND, NY 10304
Phone: 718-979-9191

HEARTHS A FIRE
7352 STATE HWY 23
ONEONTA, NY 13820
Phone: 607-436-9549

FIREPLACE STORE
3540 MERRICK RD
SEAFORD, NY 11783
Phone: 516-785-0047

SIGMA ENVIRONMENTAL
SYSTEMS INC
4 DELAVERGNE AVE
WAPPINGERS FALLS,
NY 12590
Phone: 845-297-4000

BOCKS WOODSTOVES & FURNACE
5763 EAST MAIN ROAD
BROCTON, NY 14716
Phone: 716-792-4419

POTTER HEATING
123 MAIN STREET
CANADAQUIA, NY 14424
Phone: 585-393-9410

CORNING NATURAL GAS
330 W. WILLIAM ST.
CORNING, NY 14830
Phone: 607-936-3755

HEARTH & HOME
6701 MANLIUS CENTER RD
E. SYRACUSE, NY 13057
Phone: 315-434-9839

CORNING NATURAL GAS
1100 CLEMENS PARKWAY
ELMIRA, NY 14901
NORTHERN SCAPES
2990 ROUTE 26 NORTH
GLEN AUBREY, NY 13777
Phone: 607-862-3630

HEARTH & HOME
726 WEST COURT ST
ITHACA, NY 14850
Phone: 607-273-3012

JAMESTOWN
HEATING & AIR SYST
1279 E SECOND ST
JAMESTOWN, NY 14701
Phone: 716-488-8275

STRENKOSKI BROS.
CONSTRUCTION
8888 PORTER RD
NIAGARA FALLS, NY 14304
Phone: 716-297-8221

ACE SWIM & LEISURE
610 NORTH GREECE ROAD
NORTH GREECE, NY 14515
Phone: 716-392-8300

VILLAGE FIREPLACE
3726 N BUFFALO RD
ORCHARD PARK, NY 14127
Phone: 716-667-6967

CENTRAL FIREPLACE
& KITCHENS
5525 TRANSIT RD
WILLIAMSVILLE, NY 14221
Phone: 716-636-9753

NEW FOUNDLAND

HEARTH TECHNOL
TORONTO
6411 EDWARDS BLVD
MISSISSAUGA, ON L5T 2P7
Phone: 905-696-9991

NORTH CAROLINA

FIRE PLACE PATIO
AND GRILL CENTER
487 CORBAN AVENUE
CONCORD, NC 28026-0327
Phone: 704-782-7213

SUNRISE
APPLIANCE CENTER
2315 CATAWABA VALLEY BLVD
HICKORY, NC 28602
Phone: 828-327-9947

CHIMNEY MASTERS
657 OCEAN HWY S
HERTFORD, NC 27944
Phone: 252-426-1426

NORTH DAKOTA

HOME HEATING-PLUMBING
701 28TH ST. SW
FARGO, ND 58106
Phone: 701-232-2541

CORANADO PRODUCTS
3709 MEMORIAL HIWY
MANDAN, ND 58554
Phone: 701-663-7902

CORANADO PRODUCTS
1150 3RD AVE W
DICKINSON, ND 58601
Phone: 701-227-8441

SCHMITTYS
PLUMBING & HEATING
942 11TH AVE S
WAHPETON, ND 58074
Phone: 701-642-6574

OHIO

NORTH CENTRAL
INSULATION INC
7539 ST RT 13 SOUTH
BELLVILLE, OH 44813
Phone: 419-886-2030

CUSTOM FIREPLACE
5537 WHIPPLE AVE NW
NORTH CANTON, OH 44720
Phone: 330-499-7341

A W ROBERT & SON
505-521 E PERKINS AVE
SANDUSKY, OH 44870
Phone: 419-626-3178

OVERHEAD DOOR
COMPANY OF TOLEDO
1621 W ALEXIS RD
TOLEDO, OH 43612
Phone: 419-476-0300

BUSH'S QUALITY
FIREPLACE
11216 GLADSTONE RD
WARREN, OH 44481
Phone: 330-538-2367

DAYTON FIREPLACE
SYSTEMS INC.
450 GARGRAVE RD
WEST CARROLLTON,
OH 45449
Phone: 937-847-8139

DAVID WHITE SERVICES
5315 HEBBARDSVILLE RD
ATHENS, OH 45701
Phone: 740-594-8381

THE GAS
CONNECTION INC
9900 E WASHINGTON ST
BAINBRIDGE, OH 44023
Phone: 440-543-7386

PARADISE COVE
1220 W WOOSTER
BOWLING GREEN, OH 43402
Phone: 419-352-7776

YOUNGSTOWN PROPANE
4445 BOARDMAN
CANFIELD RD
CANFIELD, OH 44406
Phone: 330-702-0800

J M S MECHANICAL
127 E INDIANA ST
EDGERTON, OH 43517
Phone: 419-298-2701

DAVID WHITE SERVICES
1257 SUGAR GROVE RD
LANCASTER, OH 43130
Phone: 740-654-4328

HEAT EXCHANGE
34205 LORRAIN RD
N. RIDGEVILLE, OH 44039
Phone: 440-327-6242

COUNTRY STOVE
6669 ROYALTON RD
NORTH ROYALTON,
OH 44133
Phone: 440-582-0062

BUSY BEAR
FIREPLACE & PATIO SHOP
533 SOUTH GREEN RD
SOUTH EUCLID, OH 44121
Phone: 216-291-5585

YOUNGSTOWN PROPANE
810 N MERIDAN RD
YOUNGSTOWN, OH 44509
Phone: 330-792-6571

JENNINGS HEATING CO INC
1671 E MARKET ST
AKRON, OH 44305
Phone: 330-784-1286

KERNS FIREPLACE
5217 TAMA RD
CELINA, OH 45822
Phone: 419-363-2230

OKLAHOMA

RICKS LAWN & HEARTH
333 W BRITTON RD
OKLAHOMA CITY,
OK 73114
Phone: 405-843-5589

ONTARIO

HEARTHLAND FIREPLACES LIMITED
5450 MAINWAY DR.
BURLINGTON, ON L7L 6A4
Phone: 905-319-0474

HEARTH TECHNOLOGIES
6411 EDWARDS BLVD
MISSISSAUGA, ON L5T 2P7
Phone: 905-696-9991

ONTARIO HEARTH LTD
3585 LAIRD RD UNIT #2
MISSISSAUGA, ON L5L 5Z8
Phone: 905-569-2404

FIREPLACE 2000 INC
27 DUFFLAW RD
TORONTO, ON M6A 2W2
Phone: 416-782-3500

MARSHS STOVE
& FIREPLACES
3322 DUNDAS ST W
TORONTO, ON M6P 2A4
Phone: 416-762-4582

FINELINE GAS FIREPLACES
90 FROBISHER DR
UNIT A
WATERLOO, ON N2V 2A1
Phone: 519-725-3055

YANCH HEATING
41 COMMERCE PARK DR
UNIT A
BARRIE, ON L4M 4S7
Phone: 705-728-5406

ONTARIO GAS
21 KENVIEW BLVD
UNIT 5
BRAMPTON, ON L6T 5G7
Phone: 905-793-1555

COUNTRY HEARTH
& CHIMNEY RR 4
7650 HWY 2
COBOURG, ON K9A 4J7
Phone: 905-372-0223

GROSSI HEATING & COOLING
238 TALBOT ST WEST
LEAMINGTON,
ON N8H 1P1
Phone: 519-326-901

WISMERS HEATING
& COOLING LIMITED
305 CRANSTON CRES
MIDLAND, ON L4R 4P4
Phone: 705-526-4188

APPLEWOOD AIR COND.
3525 HAWKESTONE RD
MISSISSAUGA, ON L5C 2VI
Phone: 905-275-4500

CANCO ELECTRIC
HEATING & AIR COND
1235 GORHAM ST
UNIT 13
NEW MARKET,
ON L3Y 7V1
Phone: 905-898-3912

EVANS REFRIGERATION
4065 STANLEY AVE
NIAGRA FALLS, ON L2E 4Z1

KAWARTHA FIREPLACES
765 THE KINGSWAY
PETERBOROUGH,
ON K9J 6W7
Phone: 705-741-1900

LAMBTON HEATING
809 MICHIGAN AVE
SARINA, ON N7V 1H1
Phone: 519-344-5521

KASTLE FIREPLACE
1960 ELLESMERE RD
SCARBOROUGH,
ON M1H 2V9
Phone: 416-289-0009

MARQUIS FIREPLACE
1825 MANNING RD
TECUMSEH, ON N8N 2L9
Phone: 519-979-6025

A TOUCH OF CLASS
665 MILLWAY AVE UNIT #8
CONCORD, ON L4K 3T8
Phone: 905-761-7111

THE WOODBURNER LEISURE CENTRE
396 VICTORIA ST NORTH
KITCHENER, ON N2H 5E6
Phone: 519-578-9663

JUNCTION FIREPLACE
BROWNVILLE JUNCTION P
17250 HWY 27
SCHOMBERG, ON L0G 1T0
Phone: 905-939-2484

KASTLE FIREPLACE LTD
12555 TENTH LINE
STOUFFVILLE, ON L4A 7Z6
Phone: 905-472-9432 Fax: 905-294-7058

MANTELS PLUS GAS FIREPLACE FACTORY
96 RANKIN ST SUITE 102
WATERLOO, ON N2V 1V9
Phone: 519-746-5355

JERRYS HEATING
RR2
CARRYING PLACE, ON K0K 1L0
Phone: 613-965-6381 Fax: 613-965-1815

NORTHERN COMFORT & MECHANICAL
20 BALSAM ST UNIT 17A
COLLINGWOOD, ON L9Y 4H7
Phone: 705-445-5670

COSTELLOE & ASSOCIATES
391 EDGELEY BLVD. #19
CONCORD, ON L4K 4A7
Phone: 905-709-2387

SIPCO ENERGIES
90 ADVANCE RD
ETOBICOKE, ON M8Z 2T7
Phone: 416-233-4820

KLOMPMAKERS
HEATING & A/C
2490 MARSDALE DR
PETERBOROUGH, ON K9L 1R4
Phone: 705-741-3922

THE FIREPLACE SHOP
379 EGLINGTON AVE WEST
TORONTO, ON M5N 1A3
Phone: 416-483-1443

OREGON

MOUNTAIN VIEW HEATING
475 SE BRIDGEFORD
BEND, OR 97702
Phone: 541-389-6714

ADVANCED AIR & METAL INC.
691 EAST VILAS ROAD
CENTRAL POINT, OR 97502
Phone: 541-772-6866

TRI COUNTY TEMP CONTROL
13150 S CLACKAMAS RIVER DR
OREGON CITY, OR 97045
Phone: 503-557-2220

JAHNKE HEATING & AIR CONDITIONING
112 S PACIFIC HWY
TALENT, OR 97540
Phone: 541-779-8496

DIAMOND HEATING
BASIN ST & INDUSTRIAL
ASTORIA, OR 97103
Phone: 503-325-7932

CORVALLIS HEATING
1557 SE CRYSTAL LAKE DR
CORVALLIS, OR 97333
Phone: 541-753-4328

MIDDLETON HEATING SHEET METAL
610 WASHINGTON AVE
CORVALLIS, OR 97333
Phone: 541-758-3358

HOME COMFORT
1827 S MAIN
DALLAS, OR 97338
Phone: 503-623-2341

FIREPLACE SHOWCASE
1601 SE RIVER ROAD
HILLSBORO, OR 97123
Phone: 503-693-7532

GROTH-GATES HEATING & SHEET METAL
2614 SE HWY 101
LINCOLN CITY, OR 97367
Phone: 541-994-2631

STARDUCT
18301 SOUTH CADLE RD
OREGON CITY, OR 97045
Phone: 971-570-3866

EASTSIDE HEATING
7200 SE JOHNSON CREEK BLVD
PORTLAND, OR 97206
Phone: 503-774-3281

FIRESIDE DIST OF OREGON INC
18389 SW BOONES FERRY RD
PORTLAND, OR 97224
Phone: 503-684-8535

LISACS SPARK & SPLASH
12518 NE AIRPORT WAY STE 155
PORTLAND, OR 97230
Phone: 503-261-1000

NW NATURAL APPLIANCE CENTER
2610 SE 8TH AVE
PORTLAND, OR 97202
Phone: 503-220-2362

HOME FIRE STOVE SHOP
1695 MARKET ST NE
SALEM, OR 97301
Phone: 503-694-6339

MARSHALLS INC
4110 OLYMPIC ST
SPRINGFIELD, OR 97478
Phone: 541-747-7445

HOT SPOT
11525 SW CANYON RD
BEAVERTON, OR 97005
Phone: 503-626-4652

UNITED MECHANICAL CONTRACTORS INC
2219 WASHBURN WAY
KLAMATH FALLS,
OR 97603
Phone: 541-884-1521

RELIABLE HEATING
2222 MAIN ST
SWEET HOME, OR 97386
Phone: 503-367-8706

PENNSYLVANIA

AMBLER FIREPLACE
& PATIO
791 BETHLEHEM PIKE
COLMAR, PA 18915
Phone: 215-997-7300

VILLAGE FIREPLACE
251 MILL ST
DANVILLE, PA 17821
Phone: 570-271-1869

SALTERS FIREPLACE
& STOVE INC
3130 RIDGE PIKE
EAGLEVILLE, PA 19403
Phone: 610-631-9372

WOODY'S FIREPLACE
323 GRANDVIEW AVE RT 6
HONESDALE, PA 18431
Phone: 800-468-7855

SEASON HEARTH & PATIO
1060 GREELEY AVE
IVYLAND, PA 18974
Phone: 215-442-0600

WOODY'S FIREPLACE
130 NARROWS RD
LARKSVILLE, PA 18651
Phone: 570-283-2534

FIREPLACE & PATIOPLACE
4680 OLD WM PENN HY
MONROEVILLE, PA 15146
Phone: 412-372-3011

FIREPLACE & PATIOPLACE
SOUTH HILLS
1651 MC FARLAND RD
PITTSBURGH, PA 15216
Phone: 412-343-5157

FIREPLACE & PATIOPLACE
4920 MC KNIGHT RD
PITTSBURGH, PA 15237
Phone: 412-366-6970

WOOD HEAT
1924 RT 212
PLEASANT VALLEY
QUAKERTOWN, PA 18951
Phone: 610-346-7894

S & T COOMBE
P O BOX 599
BLAKESLEE, PA 18610
Phone: 570-646-8254

KOHLHEPP TRUE VALUE
650 DUBOIS ST
DUBOIS, PA 15801
Phone: 814-371-5200

HOWELL CRAFT INC
591 SIMPSON HOWELL RD
ELIZABETH, PA 15037
Phone: 412-751-6861

FERRIERS FIREPLACE
2827 W 26TH ST
ERIE, PA 16506
Phone: 814-833-1234

GHAC HEATING
& AIR CONDITIONING
112 MAIN ST
GREENVILLE, PA 16125
Phone: 724-588-2120

CONCORD PLUMBING
& HEATING INC
116 CLINTON ST
NORTH EAST, PA 16428
Phone: 814-725-9812

HELLERS GAS & FIREPLACE
589 E 7TH ST
BLOOMSBURG, PA 17815
Phone: 570-784-8410

SHORTS STOVES
CHIMNEYS, & FIREPLACES
1601 ELIZABETH AVE
LAURELDALE, PA 19605
Phone: 610-929-1813

A.E.S. HEARTHPLACE INC.
1743 PINE RD
NEWVILLE, PA 17241
Phone: 717-486-7690

GLICK ASSOCIATES
P O BOX 69
SHAMOKIN DAM,
PA 17876-0069
Phone: 570-743-7332

WESS ENERGY
SAVINGS SYSTEMS
1611 NEW GERMANY RD
SUMMERHILL, PA 15958
Phone: 814-495-9912

R E SMITH CO
1217 W 4TH ST
WILLIAMSPORT, PA 17701
Phone: 570-323-4123

COUNTRY COMFORT.
3945 W MARKET ST
YORK, PA 17404
Phone: 717-792-9634

KILLIAN FIREPLACE
4303 CARLISLE PIKE
CAMP HILL, PA 17011
Phone: 717-761-1617

GAS WORKS
108 LANCASTER AVE
FRAZER, PA 19355
Phone: 610-296-3557

COMFORT ONE SYSTEMS INC
990 BALTIMORE PIKE
GLEN MILLS, PA 19342
Phone: 610-459-4665

W L STERNER INC
516 FREDERICK ST
HANOVER, PA 17331
Phone: 717-637-2159

ADVANCE AIR HEATING
& HEARTHS INC.
49 MAIN ST
LAWRENCEVILLE, PA 16929
Phone: 570-827-3277

21ST CENTURY FIREPLACES
35 OAK HILL
PARADISE, PA 17562
Phone: 717-687-3509

HADESTY HARDWARE
23RD & W MARKET ST
POTTSVILLE, PA 17901
Phone: 570-628-4300

QUEBEC

HEARTH TECHNOLOGIES
6411 EDWARDS BLVD
MISSISSAUGA, ON L5T 2P7
Phone: 905-696-9991

FOYER DESIGN
803.CURE LABELLE
BLAINVILLE, PQ J7C 3P5
Phone: 450-979-6650

DISTRIBUTION GAJ
299A BUOL DAN JOU
CHATEAUGAY, PQ J6J 2R5
Phone: 450-691-5636

DECOR CHALEUR
2055 BOUL LABELLE
LA FONTAINE, PQ J7Y 1S6
Phone: 450-438-3513

POMERLEAU GAS
5 RUE SHERBROOKE
MAGOG, PQ J1X 2A4
Phone: 819-843-3344

PROPANE ACTION
115 DES RUISSEAUX
MARIEVILLE, PQ J3M-1P7
Phone: 450-460-3900

BOUTIQUE RELAXE
FLAMME INC
2860 COTE RICHELIEU
TROIS-RIVIERES OUEST,
PQ G8Z 3Y5
Phone: 819-372-0970

RHODE ISLAND

STOVEPIPE
FIREPLACE SHOP
654 WARWICK AVE
WARWICK, RI 02888
Phone: 401-941-9333

SASKATCHEWAN

NORTHERN FIREPLACE
140 6TH AVE EAST
REGINA, SK S4N 5A5
Phone: 306-781-8007

NORTHERN FIREPLACE
1701 SASKATCHEWAN AVE
SASKATOON, SK S7K 1P7
Phone: 306-244-2774

SOUTH CAROLINA

FIRESIDE
HEARTH & HOME
1091 THOUSAND OAKS
GOLDEN OAKS
BUSINESS PARK
GREENVILLE, SC 29607
Phone: 864-281-0755

CHARLESTON
FIREPLACES
7138 B CROSS
COUNTRY ROAD
NO CHARLESTON, SC 29418
Phone: 843-767-0079

FIRESIDE
HEARTH & HOME
3375 ASHLEY
PHOSPHATE RD NO
CHARLESTON, SC 29418
Phone: 843-552-3737

SOUTH DAKOTA

FIREPLACE
PROFESSIONALS, INC
1217 W 41ST ST
SIOUX FALLS, SD 57105
Phone: 605-339-0775

BRICK PROPANE INC
721 S STATE ST
ABERDEEN, SD 57401
Phone: 605-225-6383

UNITED BUILDING CTR
920 9TH AVE SW
WATERTOWN, SD 57201
Phone: 605-886-2103

KAISER HEATING
& COOLING
808 W 23RD ST
YANKTON, SD 57078
Phone: 605-665-2895

FARMER'S PROPANE
303 ELM ST
ARLINGTON, SD 57212
Phone: 605-983-5621

HOMESTEAD
DO-IT CENTER
823 MAIN AVE S
BROOKINGS, SD 57006
Phone: 605-692-6191

UNITED BUILDING
445 N 4TH ST NW
RR 2 BOX 148A
HURON, SD 57350
Phone: 605-352-9382

TENNESSEE

BMC SALES #2 MEMPHIS
8271 INDUSTRIAL DRIVE
OLIVE BRANCH, TN 38654
Phone: 662-895-243

AMERICAN FIREPLACE
241 W MAIN STREET
SEVIERVILLE, TN 37862
Phone: 865-429-3377

TEXAS

PARRISH AND COMPANY
3600 KIPHEN RD
ROUND ROCK, TX 78664
Phone: 512-835-0937

PERFECTION
WHOLESALE
6742 N. ELDRIDGE
HOUSTON, TX 77041
Phone: 713-937-4575

PARRISH & COMPANY
26995 HWY 281 N
SAN ANTONIO, TX 78260
Phone: 830-980-9595

UTAH

BILLS COMFORT SYSTEM
159 S MAIN
LAYTON, UT 84041
Phone: 801-544-4261

FIREPLACE ETC.
560 SOUTH UNIVRSTY AVE
PROVO, UT 84604
Phone: 801-375-5787

BEEHIVE BRICK
298 MERCER WAY
SALT LAKE CITY, UT 84115
Phone: 801-355-3475

VERMONT

CHIMNEY SWEEP
FIREPLACE SHOP
3113 SHELBURNE RD
SHELBURNE, VT 05482
Phone: 802-985-4900

PROCTOR GAS INC
2 MARKET ST
PROCTOR, VT 05765
Phone: 802-459-3340

HOME COMFORT
WAREHOUSE
P O 4289 1401 RT 14
WHITE RIVER JNCTN,
VT 05001
Phone: 802-295-8778

FRIENDS OF THE SUN
159 DEPOT STREET
MANCHESTER, VT 05255
Phone: 802-362-4070

VIRGINIA

FIREPLACE SHOP
EASY FIRE SUPPLY
16165 SHADY GROVE RD
GAITHERSBURG, MD 20877
Phone: 301-990-6195

FIRESIDE HEARTH
& HOME
2227 DABNEY RD
RICHMOND, VA 23230
Phone: 804-278-6170

HEARTHSIDE
FIREPLACE
7149 HWY 58 W
CLARKSVILLE, VA 23927
Phone: 434-374-9000

WOODBURNERS TWO
6600 ARLINGTON BLVD
FALLS CHURCH, VA 22042
Phone: 703-241-1400

WASHINGTON

FIRESIDE INC.
18862 72ND AVE S
KENT, WA 98032
Phone: 425-251-9447

HANDYS HEATING
17737 STATE ROUTE 536
MOUNT VERNON,
WA 98273
Phone: 360-428-0969

ISLAND HEATING
630 WEST INDUSTRIAL
OAK HARBOR, WA 98277
Phone: 360-679-1900

OLYMPIA FIREPLACE
SUPPLY, INC.
506 E 4TH AVE
OLYMPIA, WA 98501
Phone: 360-352-4328

CAMPBELL & BRUCE
2828 W IRVING
PASCO, WA 99301
Phone: 509-545-9848

SUNSET AIR
110 E ROBERT BUSH DR
SOUTH BEND, WA 98586
Phone: 360-875-4070

WEST VIRGINIA

FIRESIDE AND
PATIO SHOP
804 CROSS LANES DR
CROSS LANES
CHARLESTON, WV 25313
Phone: 304-776-3546

WARNERS STOVE SHOP
1201 VIRGINIA AVE
CUMBERLAND, WV 21502
Phone: 301-724-0774

FAULKNER
HEARTH AND HOME
3912 MURDOCK AVE
PARKERSBURG, WV 26101
Phone: 304-424-6200

TOP HAT STOVES
& POOLS
2258 MAIN ST
WHEELING, WV 26003
Phone: 304-233-6262

WISCONSIN

THE FIREPLACE
CORNER
5688 MILLR TRNK HWY
DULUTH, MN 55811
Phone: 218-729-4895

FIRESIDE
HEARTH & HOME
3235 DENMARK AVE
EAGAN, MN 55121
Phone: 651-452-3399

FIRESIDE
HEARTH & HOME
310 WESTHILL BLVD
APPLETON, WI 54914
Phone: 920-733-4911

BUECHEL STONE
N 4399 HWY 175 SOUTH
FOND DU LAC, WI 54935
Phone: 414-922-4790

HEARTHSIDE WAUKESHA
1501C PARAMOUNT DR
WAUKESHA, WI 53186
Phone: 262-896-3774

MARCELL'S
1810 6TH ST
WAUSAU, WI 54403
Phone: 715-848-5194

FIRESIDE HEARTH
& HOME ROSEVILLE
2700 N FAIRVIEW AVE
ROSEVILLE, MN 55113
Phone: 651-633-1042

FIRESIDE
HEARTH & HOME
2540 HASTINGS WAY
EAU CLAIR, WI 54701
Phone: 715-832-5232

PROFESSIONAL HEATING
2944 HOLMGREN WAY
GREEN BAY, WI 54304
Phone: 414-336-0110

NORTHWOODS STOVE AND FIREPLACE
10544 MAIN
HAYWARD, WI 54843
Phone: 715-934-4328

HEARTH & HOME DESIGN CENTER
1714 CRESTVIEW DR
HUDSON, WI 54016
Phone: 715-381-6955

LACROSSE FIREPLACE CO
5154 MRMN COULEE RD.
LACROSSE, WI 54601
Phone: 608-788-7200

HOUSE OF
HEATING INC.
1602 NORTH CENTRAL
MARSHFIELD, WI 54449
Phone: 715-384-3163

BACHMANN POOLS
& SPAS OF JANESVILLE
2821 MILTON AVE
JANESVILLE, WI 53545
Phone: 608-754-4888

PARLOR STOVES
& FIREPLACES
736 MAIN STREET
MARINETTE, WI 54143
Phone: 715-735-3130

COPY CAT
HEARTH & HOME
26500 LAKELAND AVE. N.
WEBSTER, WI 54893
Phone: 715-866-4280

WYOMING

CLIMATE CONTROL
OF JACKSON INC.
BOX 13814 890 S HWY 89
#5 HUFF LANE
JACKSON, WY 83002
Phone: 307-734-8210

D & J HEARTH
& HOME
3151 NATIONWAY #I
CHEYENNE, WY 82001
Phone: 307-638-4543

OUR THANKS
TO THESE SUPPLIERS:

BRICKSTONE STUDIOS
2108 South 38th St.
Lincoln, Nebraska 68506
(800) 449-6599

HEAT-N-GLO PRODUCTS
6665 W. Hwy 13
Minneapolis, MN 55378
(612) 890-8367
(612) 890-3525 (Fax)
info@heatnglo.com

STONE MAGIC
301 Pleasant Drive
Dallas, TX 75217
(800) 398-1199
(214) 398-1293 (FAX)

SUPERIOR CLAY CORP
Uhrichsville, Ohio
(800) 848-6166

SUPERIOR FIREPLACE CO
4325 Artesia Ave.
Fullerton, California 92633
(714) 521-7302

WALLY LITTLE WORKSHOP
4290 Carolyn Dr.
Las Vegas, Nevada 89103
(702) 367-6775

WOHNERS INC.
29 Bergen St.
Englewood, New Jersey 07631
(201) 568-7307
(201) 568-7415 (FAX)